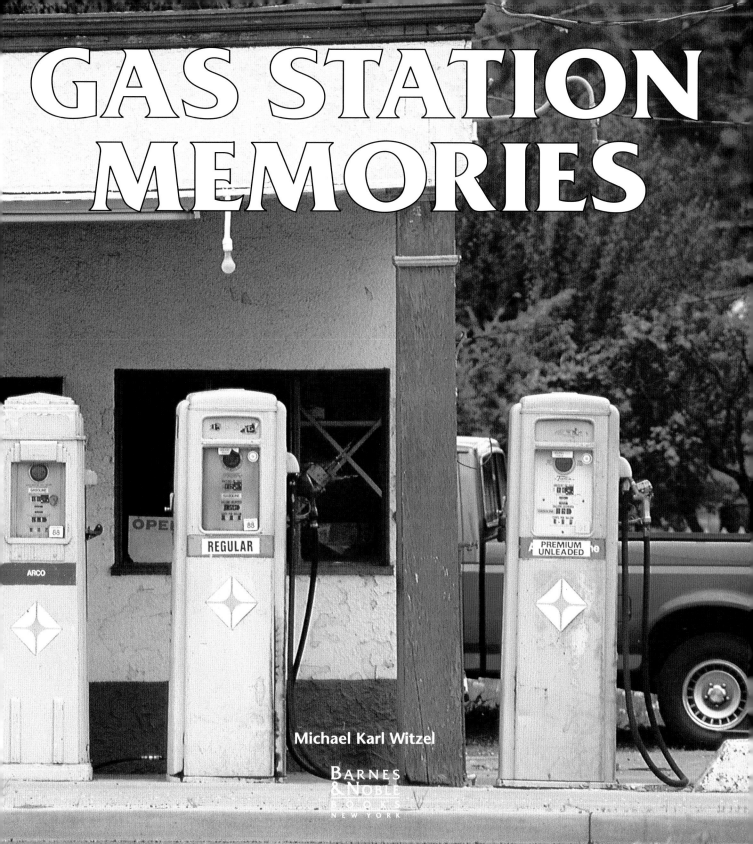

GAS STATION MEMORIES

Michael Karl Witzel

BARNES & NOBLE BOOKS
NEW YORK

This edition published by Barnes & Noble, Inc.,
by arrangement with Motorbooks International
Publishers

1998 Barnes & Noble Books

M 10 9 8 7 6 5 4

ISBN 0-7607-0795-2

First published in 1994 by Motorbooks International
Publishers & Wholesalers

Library of Congress Cataloging-in-Publication Data
Available

On the front cover: Ed Ramseier and his classic Texaco
Station as it was on U.S. 36, Idalia, Colorado. A decade
ago, it was a local roadside attraction and tourist stop,
admired by thousands of highway travelers motoring
across the United States. Today, it lies dormant—
another casualty of change. The globes that once
graced the tops of the fifties style pumps are gone.
Only the glass "Sky Chief" and "Ethyl" placards
remain. Faded paint and torn up nail-holes highlight
the spots where signs and fixtures have been hastily
removed. Once picture perfect, the crumbling
remnants remind us of values that once permeated the
American service sector. ©Larry Shirkey, 1994

On the frontispiece: In 1927, Phillips's original
corporate logo started as a disk-shaped shield
containing the "Phillips" name—along with the words
"gasoline" and "motor oil." It wasn't until 1928 that
Phillips actually incorporated the "66" designation into
their standard signage. The round version was used
until 1930, when a new "Mac West" shape was
adopted, fashioned in the shape of a six-pointed shield
as seen on national highway markers and maps. The
bright orange shield represented a familiar icon that
America trusted: it was the badge of the police officer,
stamp of approval, and sign guiding us home. Selling
gas would suit it fine, well into the future.

On the title page: Floyd Wippel manned the gas
dispensers at his Ellensburg gas station for over 42
years. While others were busy being born, going
through school, or planning lives—Wippel's service
station had remained unchanged. It's as if the passage
of time was suspended for this one roadside parcel of
ground in Washington State. Even the row of six
vintage pumping units remained to serve the unique
operation until its final days. Sadly, Mr. Wippel's small
town gasoline business closed for business a short
while ago. Although the friendly Mr. Wippel has passed
from this earthly realm, we will always remember the
way he greeted us, the quaint stories he told, and how
effortlessly he pumped gasoline.

On the back cover: During the 1940s, the
responsibility of filling an automobile gasoline tank
with motor fuel, checking the engine oil level, and
cleaning the windshield fell on one person: the service
station attendant. When it came to gasoline grades, he
knew it all. If a tire was flat and needed repair, he
patched it—right on the spot. Dressed in company
uniform and almost always wearing an eight-point
garage cap, the friendly neighborhood pump operator
was widely respected as America's automotive sage.
*Photograph provided, and reprinted with permission, by
Chevron Corporation and its subsidiary, Chevron U.S.A.
Inc., Hand-tinting by Michael Karl Witzel.*

Printed in China

CONTENTS

Dedication

Gas Station Memories is dedicated to all the unknown petroleum company staff photographers, documentary image makers, and hired shooters who never quite received their fair share of accolades. With work stored in photographic archives and company historical files, these visionary camera men and women continue to illuminate the past as recorders of streetside history. Through their discerning eyes—and by means of the silver-halide crystal—modern historians may glimpse highlights of yesterday's classic gas stations. For all those who cherish the early years of the American filling station and the golden age of the automobile, these pictures are worth a thousand words.

ACKNOWLEDGMENTS

Many thanks to the organizations that assisted. A wipe-the-windows smile to The American Petroleum Institute; Atlantic Richfield; Bennett Pump Co.; Chevron Corp.; Circa Research & Reference; the Don Garlits Museum; Gilbarco, Inc.; Michael Garman Productions; Mobil Oil Corp.; Phillips Petroleum Co.; The PoweRoyal Co.; Shell Oil Co.; Texaco Inc.; Tokheim Corp.; and the University of Louisville Ekstrom Library.

Additional thanks to all those specialists working under the hood, including Judy Ashelin; Bill Carner; Douglas Elmets; Robert Finney; Mark Frutchey; Kathy Holland; Joan Johnson; Mary Keane; David LeBeau; Dottie McKenna; Marsha Meyer; Rita Simon; Thomas Thompson; and Cherie Voris.

An attendant's salute to Tom Allen; Warren Anderson; Kent Bash; Scott Benjamin; Billie and Bob Butler; Pat Chappell; C. J. Conner; Jim and Mary Edds; Wayne Henderson; Jerry Keyser; Marty Lineen, Jr.; Frank J. Liska; Ed Love; Jeff Pedersen; Steve Perrault; Hal Polsen; Andrea and David Priebe; Howard B. Ramsay; Gary Rawlings; Steve Smith; Peter Tytla; and Walter Webber.

Special high-octane thanks to Gyvel Young-Witzel for her assistance; Clare Patterson's Red Horse Museum; and Robert McCalla and staff at the White Eagle Mall. Before the tank is full, I straighten my bowtie for Motorbooks editor Michael Dregni, for suggesting this publication and guiding it to the pumps.

INTRODUCTION

In America, gasoline stations are the type of businesses that exist mostly in the fringes of our recollection.

We love our automobiles and think nothing of carrying on talking for hours and hours about the drive we took to the top of Pikes Peak or the kicks we got on Route 66. Convertibles, steel-belted radials, fuel-injection, and the latest advancements in speed and comfort are all appropriate topics of discussion.

Yet when the point of conversation turns to refueling stations, the majority of modern-day motorists clam up. Recent controversies over environmental accidents have cast petroleum refiners in an unfavorable light. News reports exposing the inaccurate measuring practices of a few dishonest operators have compounded the image problem. To make matters worse, federal programs funded by fuel levies continue to promise higher prices at the pumps.

It's no wonder that America's unromantic refueling stations have been taken for granted. They have been a purely utilitarian necessity. But today, as the global transmutation of trade, government, and custom threatens to homogenize the world, a nation of unique individuals pines away for the "good old days." Cultural institutions with truly American roots are viewed with nostalgia. As advancing technology forces the recollections of yesteryear out from the shadows, the golden history of the gas station is being rediscovered.

Today, the naive icons of an innocent age are perceived with new vision. The specter of planetary oil depletion and the phasing out of the internal-combustion engine hover before us in the near future. Suddenly the gas station signs, gasoline dispensers, advertising images, maps, toys, and a multitude of other items once foolishly disregarded are now treasured keepsakes.

MELLOWED 80 MILLION YEARS

While brutes were hatched from eggs in OKLAHOMA

Deep in Oklahoma lie the producing sands of the Cambrian and Ordovician Ages—in some places more than a mile below the surface. Out of them comes the rich Cambro-Ordovician crude oil which is refined and blended into Sinclair Opaline Motor Oil—crude oil which had already mellowed for millions of years when dinosaurs lumbered their clumsy way above its hidden reservoirs.

Being the oldest of the Mid-continent crude oils, Cambro-Ordovician crude has had the full benefit of Nature's age-long mellowing and filtering process. Together with the other

crudes with which it is blended, it averages more than 80 million years of Nature's priceless treatment.

In process of manufacture into Sinclair Opaline Motor Oil, these crudes are not only de-waxed—they are also freed from non-lubricating petroleum jelly, a process which requires chilling the oil down to as low as 60° F. below zero.

Have the nearest Sinclair dealer change your oil to Sinclair Opaline according to the Sinclair Law of Lubrication Index. You'll find that with Opaline in your crankcase you'll use

up less oil in the heat of fast driving. This is not only a direct economy; it is also an indication that there is less friction on your bearings. Engineers know that the oils which last longest lubricate best.

NOTE: *For those who prefer a Pennsylvania grade motor oil, Sinclair dealers also sell Sinclair Pennsylvania Motor Oil made 100% from the costliest Pennsylvania grade crude (mellowed a hundred million years) and de-waxed and freed from petroleum jelly at as low as 60° F. below zero. Sinclair Refining Company (Inc.), New York, N.Y.*

Copyright 1932
by Sinclair Refining Company (Inc.)

Tune in Monday evenings 36 NBC Stations   SINCLAIR MINSTRELS

SINCLAIR OPALINE MOTOR OIL

From the oldest Mid-continent crudes

REG. U.S. PAT. OFF.

Service You Will Remember

The history of the American gas station is rich with the symbols of service, speed, power, and value. Back in the "good old days," the friendly service station attendant was always ready to wipe the windows and check the oil. Friendly service was always the kind "you will remember," and products bristled with pride and claims of superiority above all others. At the same time, potent meanings were represented by the use of powerful brand names. With this unending proliferation of exciting imagery and fantastic claims, how could Americans not fall completely in love with the automobile, and more importantly, the roadside Service Station? *Michael Witzel © 1993*

In an all out effort to capture the highlights from this unpretentious past, time fragments from a bygone age are being collected, catalogued, and archived for future reference.

Our great car culture, born almost a century ago, and the gasoline stations that

Mellowed 80 Million Years Dinos

According to the organic theory, petroleum was formed during prehistoric times when vast oceans covered much of the earth's surface. As tiny plants and animals that thrived along the coastlines died, their remains eventually settled to the bottom where a variety of bacteria caused them to decay. Sedimentary particles of fine sand and mud eventually covered the plant and animal remains and formed into hard beds of rock. As layer upon layer of stone compacted the remains, the combining forces of bacteria, pressure, heat, and other natural forces caused the materials to be transformed into oil and natural gas. As time progressed, tiny droplets of oil and minute amounts of gas moved from their original mud beds into other forms of porous rock, such as sandstone or limestone. Sinclair played on this theory during the 1930s with a series of advertisements featuring dinosaurs, touting this "age-old mellowing and filtering process" provided by mother nature and the passage of time. *Courtesy Atlantic Richfield Company*

The art of being human

FROM a woman motorist comes one of our most cherished bouquets.

"Last Saturday," she writes, "I was driving through open country and a tire blew out. It was miles to the nearest garage. There was no place I could go for help.

"Cars came by—several of them. But not one stopped—until one of your big tank trucks came along. Before I so much as raised a finger, the driver saw my predicament, jumped down, and offered to help.

"In just a few minutes, he had changed the tire—and had driven off followed by my gratitude. I call that a pretty courteous and neighborly gesture for an employee of a big and busy company!"

We value this letter because, like many of its kind, it is proof that an old-established policy of this company has born fruit. That policy is this . . . courtesy to patrons is as vital as quality of product.

The five thousand men who drive Gulf tank trucks are schooled to observe certain rules of the road which are nothing more or less than common courtesy. If you drive toward a Gulf tank truck, the driver will give you all the road the truck allows. If you approach one from behind, you'll be given ample room to pass—quickly, before you wear out your horn or your temper. And if you break down on the road, there is a chance that your first offer of help will come from the driver of a Gulf tank truck.

Gulf is proud to have grown big. But it is even prouder of staying human.

GULF REFINING COMPANY

© 1934, GULF REFINING CO., PITTSBURGH, PA.

9

powered its growth have evolved into an entity more extensive than early tinkers could ever have imagined.

In itself, our mobile society cannot easily be measured or analyzed. The motorcar and its influence has so guided the development of this nation that to examine its impact from a neutral vantage point would be impossible.

Maybe someday, when all of the businesses that now sell refined petroleum have been refitted for electric battery recharge, sale of hydrogen, or some other miracle fuel

of the future, we will be able to step back and view to what extent the automobile and its gasoline-pumping companion has affected human existence.

By then, the paper of this book will have become old and brittle, the pictures printed within faded and even more unfamiliar. The new commuters of tomorrow's roadways, whatever their manner of conveyance, will eagerly browse through these images of antiquity to dream, imagine, and maybe even wonder…whatever became of those great gas stations?

Super Shell Wayne 60
Artist C.J. Conner captured art imitating life with this painting of a Wayne pump unit used as a temporary home for a pair of birds. As more and more vintage dispensing units and gas stations are retired from use, only photographs and images like these will remain to remind us of the way things were. *C.J. Conner © 1993*

Previous page
Gulf's Art of Being Human
Back in the days when physicians still visited patients in their homes, it wasn't at all unusual for Gulf's company truck drivers to assist motorists stranded along the roadways. According to advertisements of the period, drivers of Gulf tanker trucks could be counted on for courteous driving as well as spur of the moment assistance. Like their friendly counterparts at the neighborhood service station, they were eager to please and would perform any duty toward this end. Helping the hapless automobile owner without charge was the type of advertising money could not buy. For the Gulf Oil Company, this friendly service attitude was more than just a great public relations vehicle; it was an important part of "the art of being human." *Photograph provided, and reprinted with permission, by Chevron Corporation and its subsidiary, Chevron U.S.A. Inc.*

All Sold Out

Artist Peter Tytla's handmade collages are usually made up of over 200 individual photographs. His favorite place to hang out is the salvage yard, a fertile breeding ground for many of his most useful collage components. Five weeks of meticulous labor goes into each one of his humorous scenes, with each individual photograph carefully cut out, re-touched, and glued into place. As all the elements slowly come together, Tytla "begins to cook," carefully placing every photographic fragment in its proper place, as if by intuition. The resulting photographic composite becomes a frenetic jumble of automotive parts, gasoline station artifacts, and eclectic junkyard scenery. In the midst of the visual cacophony, an outspoken individual usually takes center stage. For petroliana aficionados and those bent towards the appreciation of the American road (and the junkyards that often adjoin them), Tytla's collages are truly an amazing sight to behold. (Original art 30inx40in). *Peter Tytla © 1993*

Chapter 1

STATIONS

When Laessig and Grenner formed the Automobile Gasoline Company in St. Louis, no one had to explain to the pair what was wrong with refueling an automobile. By 1905, most Missouri vehicle owners knew that powering a motorcar with gasoline was inconvenient, messy, and extremely dangerous.

So, in an effort to enhance the onerous procedure, the partnership decided to simplify it. By attaching a flexible section of hollow rubber tubing to an upright storage tank, they pumped life into a roadside ritual in dire need of improvement. The filler hose became the new standard for refueling.

Two years later, Standard Oil of California duplicated the effort by installing the first filling station of its kind on the West Coast. Incorporating the flexible hose as an important part of the operation, area sales manager John McLean inaugurated the flagship station for the new Seattle territory.

As filling a gas tank became more practical, former skeptics began to endorse the automobile. By the mid-1920s, improved roads cut a bold path across America—shifting the nation's cultural center of gravity away from the cities. By then, over 250,000 stations were pumping gas along the way.

Wippel's Gas Station, Ellensburg, Washington
About twenty years ago, every small town in America had a gasoline station like Wippel's. Today, those types of businesses are all closed, supplanted by some form of gasoline convenience store. The act of grabbing a bag of potato chips and a soft-drink (in a "Jurassic Park" commemorative cup) at the neighborhood quick-shop is a perfectly normal activity for children growing up in the modern age. The idea of yesterday's general store has been resurrected— albeit reshaped and re-formatted for a brave new world. Now, it serves an expanded roster of functions far superior to its predecessor: local teenage hangout, smoke-shop, center for individual video gaming, snack-center, touch-tone communications hub, beer and wine stockade, and a reliable place for the boys in blue to get their fresh coffee and doughnuts. Aren't the changes that progress brings a wonderful thing?

With the sale of oil and motor fuel now an established industry, refiners began to revamp their sales outlets. The disheveled image of the tumble-down gasoline shack became an economic liability. Slowly, America's unorganized rabble of refueling outposts evolved into a network of serious service stations.

Now, stately structures with all the respectability of the local bank and library were constructed along the roadsides. Polished stone and terra-cotta soon adorned service station buildings worthy of any civic office. Neo-classical architecture became the rage as many gas stations cleaned up their image.

A few bold operators experimented with more outlandish styles as filling stations assumed the shape of lighthouses, seashells, castles, windmills, and even giant gasoline pumps. To the delight of many, the Pure Oil Company constructed stations replicating small English cottages. Oil canisters replaced pies cooling on the windowsill.

As the gasoline station searched for its identity, the great depression of '29 sent prices tumbling. In some cities, the average price per gallon dropped to ten cents! 2.5 million vehicles came to a grinding halt. To bolster sagging revenues, the practice of selling tires, batteries, and accessories sud-

Early Curbside Pump, circa 1915
By 1915, virtually any business owner who wished to sell gasoline could have a pump and storage tank installed outside their shop and advertise gasoline. Because thousands of these new income-generating outlets could be easily obtained by the oil concerns in a matter of months, the need to secure new real estate was bypassed. Profits from the sale of gas could be realized in a very short time. Refiners had only to install pumps, deliver the gas, and collect their huge share of the profits. Individual shop owners would handle sales and collect the generous revenues. Within a very short amount of time, the curbside gasoline pump (such as this Tokheim Curb Post Outfit No. 14) could be seen from almost any streetside vantage point. *Courtesy Tokheim Corporation*

Moran Gas Tank Wood Dipstick
Before the widespread use of remote gasoline gauges, today's simple glance at the dashboard to check fuel level was not possible. Early station attendants and do-it-yourself motorists usually had to check their gasoline receptacle manually. For the most part, that meant inspecting the tank for fluid level and listening for the tell-tale sounds of "being full" when pumping. Of course, this practice resulted in spills and overall inconvenience, necessitating the need for a more accurate method. As a stop-gap measure until the new technology could be implemented, many stations passed out wooden "dipsticks" that allowed curious automobilists a more practical method of checking fuel level. Unfortunately, automotive tanks were not any sort of standard size, accounting for the often confusing set of scales found on these crude instruments. *White Eagle Antique Mall Collection*

The Teapot Dome Station Hut, Zilla, Washington
The "Teapot Dome" oil scandal of 1923 was a dark day for this nation's petroleum refiners as well as the administration of President Warren G. Harding. A Senate investigation uncovered that Secretary of the Interior Albert Fall had persuaded Secretary of the Navy Edwin Denby to transfer government oil reserves located at Teapot Dome, Wyoming, and Elk Hills, California, to the Department of the Interior. Mr. Fall then leased these reserves to private petroleum producers E.L. Doheny and Harry Sinclair. Absolutely no competitive bidding of any kind was involved, and the subsequent lease deals were illegally secured by the refiners with large amounts of money. As a tongue-in-cheek reminder of those infamous days, a quaint gasoline station shaped like a teapot takes care of motorists in Zilla, Washington. For the average motorist unschooled in the history of the American gas station, it's just another crazy roadside attraction vying for its share of the gasoline trade.

denly became an integral part of the service station marketing scheme.

To keep customers from patronizing other shops, stations also consolidated repair bays, lubritoriums, and tire services under one roof. Even gasoline pumps became part of the all-out merchandising effort. New fuel dispensers featured glass cabinets capable of housing motor oils, anti-freeze, head lamps, cables, and other automotive gadgetry.

16

Keeler's Korner, Lynnwood, Washington
Tall gasoline pumps with clear glass crucibles towered
over Highway 99 when Keeler's Korner first opened in
1927. In those early days of the automobile, Carl Keeler
pumped the gasoline himself and never once failed to
check the oil level in the customer's crankcase. Back
then, traveling over the highways and byways of
rural America was still quite enjoyable. Enthusiastic
automobilists (ain't we got fun) bent on experiencing
all the joys of the motorcar delighted in taking even

the smallest of journeys. Simple pleasures still
prevailed. The journey itself was the focus of almost
every trip, and the destination less important than the
fun and adventure to be had along the way! To this
day, a pair of slender red pump dispensers still draw
the curious to old man Keeler's quaint green and
white building in Lynnwood, Washington. Although
gasoline is no longer sold here, the pleasant memories
and rich recollections to be savored at Keeler's Korner
are absolutely free.

As the end of the thirties approached,
new station structures incorporated elements of Streamline Moderne. Decorative

pylons, speed lines, curved corners, neon
tubing, and portholes provided an illusion
of speed. At long last, filling stations and

Tony's Tank Standard Station, circa 1930
During the 1930s, station attendants were always on alert for the motorist. This Standard Oil outlet featured a women's restroom, three Wayne 60 gasoline dispensers, Pyro Anti-Freeze, Mobiloil, Esso lubrication products, Kyso gasoline, and of course—ice-cold Coca-Cola in bottles. If only today's station attendant looked so alert! *Courtesy Caufield & Shook Collection, Photographic Archives, University of Louisville. Neg.# CS 155188*

roadways became mutually complimentary. For a brief period in the timeline of the American gas station, commercial refueling structures attained their purest form: not Grecian monuments, Chinese Pagodas, nor country cottages ... but highly specialized businesses geared to refilling automobiles with gasoline.

Commercial Pumper House, Fredonia, Kansas

Early gasoline refueling structures were simply glorified sheds and other makeshift structures. To remain competitive and attract motorists, petroleum companies learned that a more dignified image had to be portrayed. As a result, a number of refiners chose to fashion their station buildings in the familiar house format. Pure Oil and Phillips constructed many of these cottage gasoline outlets, practically bringing the safe and secure feeling of home to the American roadways. For the oil marketer, the quaint form held another attraction: Because the house fit in so well and in some cases was regarded as an "architectural asset," restrictive zoning ordinances and construction bans were often eased. Accepted as one of the most popular forms of architecture for gas sales, the English cottage was readily accepted for installation in most suburban communities during the twenties. With its newfound respect, the gasoline station could be constructed virtually anywhere a roadside lot was available—including residential areas.

Chevron Station With Attendants, circa 1940s

During the 1940s, the responsibility of filling an automobile gasoline tank with motor fuel, checking the engine oil level, and cleaning the windshield fell on one person: the service station attendant. Dressed in company uniform and almost always wearing an eight-point garage cap, the friendly neighborhood pump operator was widely respected as America's automotive sage. When it came to gasoline grades, he knew it all. If a tire was flat and needed repair, he patched it—right on the spot. Lubrication viscosity, mile-per-gallon, and tire rotation were all subjects he (and sometimes she) could offer advice about. Regardless of his technical prowess or mechanical ability, the service station attendant wasn't afraid of hard work, checking the oil, and wiping the windshield. *Photograph provided, and reprinted with permission, by Chevron Corporation and its subsidiary, Chevron U.S.A. Inc., Hand-tinting by Michael Karl Witzel.*

Neon Station Clock

During the heyday of the American gas station, the Electric Neon Clock Company of Cleveland, Ohio, produced a number of beautiful clocks for use in service stations and other commercial roadside structures. Long before digital electronics transformed timepieces into impersonal chronometers, colorful rings of bright neon outlining bold analog clock-dials ruled the roadsides. Restaurants used them as centerpieces above their Formica counters and gas station owners proudly mounted them above the office door. Along with the familiar red Coke machine and the mirror-front cigarette machine, these colorful clocks were an accepted part of the average gas station scene. But, like everything else familiar that is quickly taken for granted, the classic neon clock fell from popularity with nary a whimper. Today, only a scarce smattering of these precious survivors remains—awaiting their rediscovery—and eventual rebirth.

20

Opposite page, bottom
Standard Oil Service Station, 1949
Standard Oil of California operated a number of eye-catching stations on the West Coast during the late'40s. Station attendants dressed in pure white conveyed a positive image to the motorist and helped to diminish the "grease monkey" reputation some auto service men inadvertently promoted. *Photograph provided, and reprinted with permission, by Chevron Corporation and its subsidiary, Chevron U.S.A. Inc.*

Phillips 66 Full Service, 1952
The true story of the Phillips company trademark began when the first gallon of gas was offered to the motoring public in Wichita, Kansas, on November 19, 1927. Phillips was venturing into the consumer market, their goal being to offer a fuel superior to any currently sold. In the frenzy to perfect their product, Phillips delayed selecting the right imagery to represent the new gas until the last minute. A special executive committee session was organized for the sole purpose of coming up with a new trademark. On the night of the meeting, a Phillips company official was returning to headquarters in Bartlesville in a company car being used to test the new Phillips gasoline. "This car goes like 60 on our new gas," the official exclaimed. "Sixty nothing," answered the driver, glancing at the speedometer, "we're doing 66!" The next day at the conference the incident was reported. Somebody asked where this actually occurred and the answer came back: "Near Tulsa on Highway 66." That locked it up! "Phillips 66" did sound pretty catchy. A vote was put to the committee and the decision came back unanimous. The new banner under which the Phillips Petroleum Company would launch its line of gasolines would be none other than "Phillips 66." The Phillips 66 trademark is viewed as one of the most widely recognized corporate symbols representing automotive fuels in America. Numerous amusing stories and unbelievable explanations have sprung up over the years attempting to explain the origin of this distinctive logo. While some of these stories are based on facts, others remain mired in myth. Still, many of these yarns have found their way into the folklore of the American service station and continue to be passed along by the average motorist—unaware of the real facts and circumstances. (Circa 1952). *Courtesy Corporate Archives, Phillips Petroleum Company*

Abandoned Roadside Station, Mannford, Oklahoma
These days, classic station scenes from our roadside past are becoming more and more infrequent. Vintage Pepsi-Cola and Dr. Pepper signs like these are now treasured collectibles, along with the particular visible register unit still intact within this frame. Taken by photographer Harold Corsini in 1946 for Standard Oil of New Jersey, this Mannford, Oklahoma, refueling stop has seen its share of use. *Courtesy Standard Oil (New Jersey) Co. Collection, Photographic Archives, University of Louisville. Neg.# SONJ 34845*

Phillips 66, Anchorage, Alaska, 1967

One of the more bizarre stories perpetuated to explain the origin of the Phillips trademark is that a company official won the company's first Texas Panhandle refinery in a dice game! The previous owner rolled "double-sixes" in an unlucky toss and lost it all! Back over the border in Bartlesville, company directors liked those unlucky boxcars so much that they decided to name the refinery's gasoline product "Phillips 66." In reality, this story originates from the Texas refinery's infamous neighbor, (the 6666 Ranch) reportedly won in a poker game with a hand of four sixes. It's a tall Texas tale, as fanciful as those describing Jackalopes and giant armadillos. (Circa 1967). *Courtesy Corporate Archives, Phillips Petroleum Company*

Stone Station Man and Pumps, Seattle, Washington

Jack Collier fondly remembers the days when his father first opened his stone gasoline station. Back then, American cars like the Packard 120 and Ford Model "A" dominated Rainier Avenue. Tall visible register gas pumps were the current trend in dispensing equipment, indicative of the latest technology. Pumped by hand crank or electric motor, powerful motor fuel would slowly fill a glass cylinder, then drain by way of gravity into the automobile gas tank. Since pumping gas was a much slower process than present day, time was plentiful for simple services like checking the oil and pressure in the tires. When problems surfaced, station mechanics assisted with even the smallest of mechanical repairs—and why not? When hoods were pulled away, simple mechanisms offered little challenge for the experienced pump jockey handy with a wrench.

FOR EVERYTHING YOUR CAR NEEDS—

Chapter 2

ATTENDANTS

During the golden age of the American service station, attendants played a pivotal role. As highly visible employees, pump operators were an extension of the brand sold. To ensure return business, their appearance had to instill a sense of quality in the mind of the motorist. Along with gasoline, the motorist was buying an image.

As gas stations became more standardized across America, the grease-monkey became an embarrassment. Oil refiners wanted to cultivate a national image and eliminate the tumble-down gasoline shacks of the early 1900s. Station employees were required to don uniforms.

Like their well-dressed counterparts in the military, the pump jockeys had to look sharp at all times. Polished leather shoes and matching shin guards became part of the new look. Jodhpur trousers worn with a matching waist-jacket were now an important part of the basic uniform as was the crisp black bow-tie.

To pull together the unified station image, the petroleum company insignia was displayed on the breast pocket of the uniform. Fashioned in the form of a metal pin or fabric patch replicating the larger sign

Mobil Station Service Attendant
As a mythical figure of the great American roadside, the service station attendant towered above them all. As depicted in this Mobil advertisement, the attendant was indeed a larger than life figure in the mind of many an automobile owner. From coast to coast, in the big cities, small towns, and even on remote highways, he was someone to turn to in a time of need. For him, pumping gasoline, checking the oil level, and making sure that the windshields were clean was only a small part of the job. Relating to people on a one-to-one basis with friendliness and compassion was much more important. The physical embodiment of the American work ethic, pioneering spirit, and "can-do" attitude, the gasoline service station attendant was at one time an important element of the roadside tapestry. We look back to these gas pumping giants with fondness, hoping for their eventual return. *Courtesy Mobil Oil Corporation*

Rose Street Attendants, Seattle, Washington

Today, only miles from the historic Seattle site where John McLean erected one of America's first filling stations, Wally Hilde continues the full-service tradition. His eager-to-satisfy team of attendants jockey to refuel cars and skillfully repair the mechanical components that keep them moving. Service men Rodger, Juan, and Ramiro routinely infuse a healthy dose of customer service into their daily tasks—the same brand of friendliness once found at the gasoline businesses of days past. At Rose Street Auto, there are no self-service pump dispensers or faceless "attendants" cloistered behind plexiglass. Real personalities take care of customers. For all concerned, it makes the all-too-frequent routine of pulling off the fast-track to have one's gas-tank filled or oil checked a more pleasant experience. Hilde learned a long time ago that the type of relationship a business has with its patrons is what brings them back, regardless of the chemical properties of gasoline sold or the technology used to pump it from underground tanks. The most expensive facilities and equipment cannot, and never will, compensate for a basic lack of customer service.

FULL BODY

CLEAN·CLEAR·PURE

"*Still plenty of oil-and body O.K.!*"

That's the answer thousands of motorists receive who use Texaco Golden Motor Oil regularly. Even after a long, hard vacation trip this pure golden oil still clings to the "stick"—still retains that famous full body which assures many more miles of safe, care-free driving.

Texaco is specially refined from carefully selected crudes *only*, with a scientific precision that no known process can improve. It is as golden pure as it looks. It is free from gummy residual tars which cause faulty valve action and sticking piston rings—free from gritty-carbon-forming elements which cause an engine to over-heat, falter and lose power.

For maximum summer motoring satisfaction stop consistently under the Texaco Red Star with the Green T. This symbol can be seen at convenient intervals along all our great national highways. The Lincoln Highway, for instance, is a Texaco Trail with Service Stations never more than an hour apart. Texaco is the only gasoline and motor oil sold in every one of our 48 States.

THE TEXAS COMPANY, TEXACO PETROLEUM PRODUCTS

TEXACO
GOLDEN MOTOR OIL

Previous page

Texaco Body Still O.K. Motor Oil

"Still plenty of oil—and body O.K.! That's the answer thousands of motorists receive who use Texaco Golden Motor Oil regularly. Even after a long, hard vacation trip this pure golden oil still clings to the stick—still retains that famous full body which assures many more miles of safe, care-free driving." In the innocent days of motoring, motor lubricants were comprised of relatively simple blends of refined petroleum. With the fields of oil production and chemical engineering still in their infancy, limited criteria were available to analyze refined products. Thermal breakdown and viscosity were terms for the future. Clean, clear, and pure dominated the printed page. *Courtesy Texaco Inc.*

Three Attendant Service Lives

Imagine pulling into a gasoline station and having your car serviced by three station attendants! For today's jaded motorist, it's the stuff dreams are made of. However, during the thirties it was no dream: Gulf stations like this example sold No-Nox Ethyl from clock-faced pumps for fourteen and a half cents per gallon. Wiping the windows, checking the oil, and topping off the fluid in the radiator was all part of the deal. (Circa 1933). *Photograph provided, and reprinted with permission, by Chevron Corporation and its subsidiary, Chevron U.S.A. Inc.*

Can I Fill Your Tank, Mister?

Lillian Larsen was one of Standard's most able station attendants during 1942. Serving the road as an important asset to the war effort, female pump operators like her became a familiar sight at the American service station. While husbands, brothers, fathers, and cousins were battling it out for our freedom (to drive when and where we wanted), wartime gasoline stations continued to operate with as much normalcy as they could. *Photograph provided, and reprinted with permission, by Chevron Corporation and its subsidiary, Chevron U.S.A. Inc.*

Selling Furniture Polish

A service station attendant points out a new furniture polish product to a female customer at a Phillips' service station during the early 1930s. To augment revenues in the days of economic downturn, petroleum refiners manufactured a number of products for sale at company stations. The American housewife was now quite adept at the controls behind the wheel and had quickly become a major economic force to be reckoned with. Furniture polish, glass cleaner, insect spray, and a number of other fluids were routinely marketed to the modern woman—right along with gasoline and oil. The station attendant often acted as an ad hoc salesman for many of these goods, giving friendly advice for their use. The time spent at the pumps provided the perfect opportunity to win over new customers. *Courtesy Corporate Archives, Phillips Petroleum Company*

Socony Attendant's Hat
Like the military man, firefighter, police officer, and postal worker, the service station attendant of the not too distant past always wore some type of head covering while pumping gas and performing related automotive tasks. Simple cloth caps were some of the first worn by station employees, followed by the black-brimmed variety much like those already adopted by numerous government service organizations. For the most part, these multi-pointed head-toppers were an image accessory—company trademarks and related brand insignias quickly attained prominence on the frontal region of the filling station chapeau. Colorful oil company logos were routinely mounted above center brim—tying together the "unified look" so intensely desired by most of the truly competitive oil concerns. The resulting look commanded attention, respect, and trust. It's no wonder that Texaco's famous slogan, "You can trust your car to the man who wears the star," was so effective in recruiting customers.
White Eagle Antique Mall Collection

Phillips 66 Stations For Families, circa 1950s
A few scientifically oriented scenarios have been perpetuated to explain the origins of the Phillips 66 name, including the unfounded tale that Phillips gasoline was sixty-six octane and that its famous "controlled volatility" feature was perfected after sixty-six laboratory tests. Unfortunately, no one really knows for sure how many actual laboratory tests were conducted to perfect the controlled volatility of "Phillips 66" gasoline. Furthermore, the technical methods for determining gasoline octane rating wouldn't even be adopted until five years after the original Phillips trademark was selected! (Circa 1950s).
Courtesy Corporate Archives, Phillips Petroleum Company

Station Attendant's Patches

Since the first gallon of gas was sold at the American filling station, the pump attendant has acted as a highly visible product representative. When motoring was still young, excited vehicle owners cared little about how the pump or depot operator was dressed. Finding gasoline was the main concern. Yet, as gasoline locomotion became more refined, standard uniforms slowly replaced stained overalls—the attire of the average gas station employee slowly evolved into a highly refined costume. To identify the pump jockey and to differentiate the brand of gas sold, insignias were permanently affixed to hats, shirts, and jackets. While the attendant pumped gas, checked oil, or wiped the windshield, the customer would see a constant reminder of exactly what brand he was purchasing. Extremely colorful, eye-catching, and often humorous, the embroidered gasoline patch was the original predecessor of today's designer label.
Walter Webber Collection

31

Lil' Phil Attendant Doll
Well aware that gasoline station collectibles are now desired by a vast market interested in nostalgia, the Phillips Petroleum Company has recently licensed a toy manufacturer to issue number one in a series of station attendant dolls. Capturing all of the whimsy contained in the original version manufactured years ago, it comes complete—packaged with a light brown Phillips' signature attendant's uniform and black-brimmed cap. While the service station attendant many motoring Americans came to know and love during the golden age of the automobile may no longer be a reality, the magic of those former days may be recaptured with one of these commemorative dolls.

Phillips Attendant Award
As an incentive to sell gasoline, portray a positive public image, and perform quality maintenance work, many oil companies bestowed awards upon their best station attendants. Phillips Petroleum of Bartlesville, Oklahoma, utilized this commanding rendition of a service employee to honor many of their top gasoline station personnel during the 1960s. Embodying the bold styling of machine age imagery with its cubist design, this golden statuette was the equivalent of a Hollywood Oscar in the world of the service station worker. Highly prized by any station attendant worth his salt, company service awards were an important aspect of building employee character. By reinforcing the idea of customer satisfaction and adherence to quality with these awards, petroleum refiners succeeded in creating a valuable pool of automotive servers. *Red Horse Museum Collection*

near the roadway, it confirmed company identity for the motorist.

Influenced heavily by the style of military uniforms, a hat typical of any "serviceman" adorned the head. Decorated with the same company identification as the jacket, it strengthened brand recognition during face to face interactions with the public.

Eventually, oil companies relaxed styles at their stations and utilized the basic jumpsuit as uniform. Covering the legs, arms, and major portions of the body, it was the perfect shell for protection against grease and dirt. The bow-tie remained standard and soft caps made from matching fabric covered the head.

Still, a uniform mode of dress and pleasant appearance wasn't the last word in customer satisfaction. Personalities became an important issue, along with a willingness to do the job right the first time and please the customer during his or her brief visit. In the days of the Packard and Duesenberg, the customer was always right.

With a courteous smile and friendly demeanor, service station attendants were expected to carry out the basic rituals

Mobil Window Spray

One of the major attractions of full service gasoline stations used to be the simple procedure of having one's windshield cleaned. Long before the engineers in Detroit even thought of spraying cleaning fluid up through tubes mounted under the windshield, the task of wiping glass clean was the exclusive domain of America's service station attendants. The standard tools of the trade to accomplish this complimentary task included the hand-held spray bottle, rubber squeegee, and lint-free shop towel. As the gallons rang out from the pump, motorists relaxed in the front seat as every trace of bugs, mud, and road film was eradicated from the glass. Watching the process proved fascinating: there was a definite technique required to perform the task efficiently, mixed with individual flair and occasional braggadocio. For those who wanted to experiment with this "service" art and try their hand at cleaning their own wind screen, Mobil offered small bottles of glass cleaner to take home. *White Eagle Antique Mall Collection*

required to ensure motoring safety and pleasure. Checking the oil and tire pressure were a large part of the job, as was checking mechanical components under the hood for signs of impending failure. Making sure the windshield was free from dirt and insects were high on the list of station chores.

When an automobile first pulled up to the pumps, the station attendant was always there to greet it. Without hesitation, the eager-to-please attendant pleasantly inquired to the amount of gasoline desired and set about the task of operating the pump. While the fuel flowed into the tank, the pump man wasted no time daydreaming. Customers were enlightened to the different grades of motor oil, automotive questions were answered, free maps and prizes were handed out, and road directions clarified.

With flawless choreography, the skilled service station attendant could complete all of these tasks, debate the chance for rain, and make it back to the filler hose with time to spare. The tank would be full, all without spilling a drop of gasoline.

Phillips Attendant Filling, 1965

One of the most common stories explaining the use of the "66" designation is that company founder Frank Phillips was sixty-six years old when he formulated the Phillips Petroleum Company. This is far from the truth, as Mr. Phillips came into this world in the year 1873 and was only forty-four years old when the company first incorporated on June 13, 1917. "Phillips 44" would have made a rather uninteresting company trademark! Another mix-up with numbers takes the form of the first-day-of-sales story. In this version, the flagship Phillips station had sold exactly 6,600 gallons of gasoline by the end of the first day's business. Supposedly, the station operator turned to a company official (who just happened to be standing nearby) and exclaimed: "Boy, 66 is our lucky number!" This could be possible, if it weren't for the fact that Phillips' first Wichita gasoline station sold 12,000 gallons that historic day. Many patrons had free five-gallon coupons, too, further reducing the quantities actually paid for. (Circa 1965). *Courtesy Corporate Archives, Phillips Petroleum Company*

Wayne Pumps Measure Gas by the Penny's Worth

.... to Guarantee Full Value for Every Cent you Pay

IF YOU NEEDED gasoline, how many gallons could you order if you had just 80c to spend? No need to figure ... just say *"80c worth, please"* and a modern Wayne Pump will fill your order to the last full penny's worth.

Modern Waynes, *the Watchdogs of your Gasoline Dollar*, measure gasoline by the penny's worth as well as the gallon ... eliminate price figuring, "eye measure" and other sources of error ... *guarantee* you Honest Measure ... and let you order by the gallon, tankful or dollar's worth, whichever you prefer.

Waynes can't make a mistake ... can't over-charge you. *With unfailing accuracy*, Wayne's patented precision meter tallies each fraction of a gallon *as it goes into your tank*. And automatically, with split-penny accuracy, Wayne's amazing mechanical brain totals the cost, cent by cent, before your eyes.

Wherever you see them, Wayne Pumps mark dealers who put your interest first. Waynes can't be started until the dials are set to zero. *They are accurate at full flow or a trickle.* They can fill your tank to the top without spilling a drop.

So look for the Wayne name and "Honest Measure" seal ... your guarantee of accuracy.

MODEL 70-C

WAYNE

THIS SALE
$100

05¾ GALLONS AT

Wayne

See YOUR Soldier!
Visit His Camp ... By Car

Your soldier boy will be mighty glad to see faces from home ... and you'll be happy to see for yourself how well he's looking, too. So plan to go soon for at least a quick visit with him, and a look at the new defenses he's helping build for America. And make the trip by car!

All the way, you'll find modern service stations waiting like familiar friends to meet every motoring need ... to provide efficient, speedy service, maps, road information, clean rest rooms ... everything they can offer to make your journey easy and pleasant.

Wayne Pump
The Watchdog of your Gasoline Dollar

"Wayne" Honest Measure"

THE (Wayne) PUMP COMPANY...FORT WAYNE, INDIANA

World's Largest Manufacturer of Gasoline Pumps ... Est. 1891

Chapter 3

PUMPS

Sylvanus F. Bowser designed the first workable gasoline pump in 1885. Initially intended to pump coal oil, it was later modified to deliver gasoline. By 1905, it was housed within a wooden storage cabinet and dubbed a "filling station" by Bowser salesman Jake Gumpper. Easy to operate, this self-measuring storage pump marked a new age for commercial fuel dispensing.

As more effective methods replaced the depot methods of tin can, chamois, and funnel, radical pump refinements followed. By 1906, John J. Tokheim perfected a compact visible and cylinder-measuring pump featuring a water-separating glass dome. Six years later, Gilbert & Barker introduced the T-8 one-gallon hand pump. Technologically superior to previous models, it was capable of delivering fifteen gallons of fuel per minute. Still, disreputable operators could rig the dial indicator to produce false readings.

As a result, the public came to view these "blind" pumps with a suspicious eye. Unable to monitor what was really flowing through the filler hose, gasoline purchasers

Wayne Honest Measure Gas Pumps
With the introduction of the mechanical calculator pump in 1932, the Wayne Pump Company gained the confidence it needed to guarantee the customer full value for every cent they paid. The eye-measurement of the visible register pumps suddenly became outmoded, as did the large dial indicators of the clock-face pumps. Freed from the mental chore of having to figure out how many gallons could be purchased for a specific monetary amount, gasoline could be sold by increments as small as a penny! The days of purchasing motor fuel by the gallon were over and a new era of customer confidence ushered in. Unfortunately, the majority of pump companies tried to dismiss the new device as something they didn't really need. Still, as more and more stations tried the new units, their popularity spread. Soon, dealers across the country demanded the advanced pumps. A few pump manufacturers introduced their own calculators, but were soon taken to court by Wayne for patent infringement. When the dust finally settled, most manufacturers of gasoline dispensers signed licensing agreements with the Wayne Pump Company.
Courtesy Wayne Pump Company

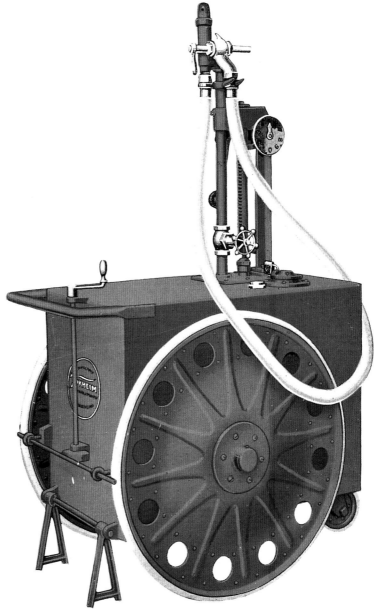

QUALITY **TOKHEIM**

Complete Filling Station Equipment,
Factory Storage and Distributing Systems

MODEL 214

PORTABLE
GASOLINE
TANK

WITH
GALLON MEASURING
PUMP

MODEL 214 Portable Unit is approved and labeled by The Underwriters' Laboratories, Inc., and is designed for safely and conveniently serving Gasoline in Garages, Service Stations, Automobile Storage or Sales Buildings, Factories and wherever stationary equipment is not advisable.

This method of handling gasoline has some advantages. When used indoors it facilitates the filling of cars without moving or shifting them, and it can be placed on the elevator and taken from floor to floor. When used at the curb it can readily be pushed indoors at night. It is sturdy and substantial and will stand severe service.

TOKHEIM OIL TANK AND PUMP COMPANY
FORT WAYNE, INDIANA, U. S. A.
Designers and Manufacturers of Complete Gasoline and Oil Dispensing Equipment

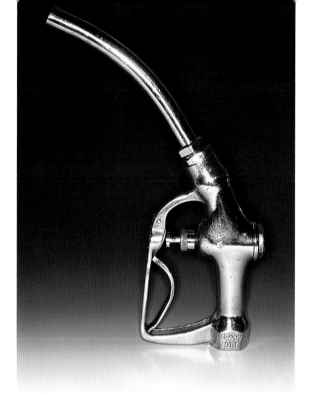

Brass Pump Handle

Gasoline pump nozzles like this brass Buckeye model were once beautiful works of utilitarian machinery. Before the advent of the information age, visual aesthetics still played an important role in the design of products, machinery, and household objects. Albeit many of these designs were considered modern for their time, they still contained that subtle hint of craftsmanship that makes an object more than the sum of its parts. Unlike today's smaller aluminum models (coated with plastic shrouds and various rubber accessories to trap vapors), these substantial valve spouts were an indispensable part of the helpful service station attendant's refueling arsenal. With pump nozzle in hand, standing at attention at the pump dressed in full-dress regalia, yesterday's gasoline station attendant was a roadside sight to behold.

Model 214 Portable Tank

The Tokheim Model 214 portable gasoline tank was a handy accessory for the early marketer of streetside gasoline. With a gallon measuring pump and internal fifty gallon storage tank, this unit could be moved easily (with its 30in wheels) to the curbside in order to service automobiles. With its use, general stores, drugstores, hardware establishments, repair facilities, and other business not normally geared to serving the motorcar with fuel could readily sell gasoline to its regular customers. One stroke of the plunger provided a full gallon, with selective stops provided for half-gallon, quart, and pint measure. A 10ft hose supplied with the unit allowed automobile gasoline tanks to be filled directly. *Courtesy Tokheim Corporation*

were highly dubious of accurate measurement and purity.

To placate beleaguered petroleum refiners and to discourage cheating, manufacturers soon introduced improved pump models. Securely mounted on top of a tall support made from heavy iron, a round glass cylinder now held gasoline in plain sight. Within the transparent crucible, graduated markers measured gas volume—plainly "registering" the amount readied for sale.

Unfortunately, the possibilities for dishonesty were not eliminated by the visible register design. A strategically placed brick could falsely inflate the measurement inside the glass cylinder. Gallon markers could easily be misaligned. Accurate readings were difficult from close angles, often rendering the motorist's view through the windshield a disadvantage.

By the close of the twenties, electric meter pumps joined the visibles on the roadside. Oversized "clock face" indicators displayed the quantity delivered on these new arrivals as a bell signaled the delivery of every gallon.

The Wayne Pump Company introduced the first calculator pumps in 1932, permanently altering the way Americans purchased gasoline. With a "Head for Figures,"

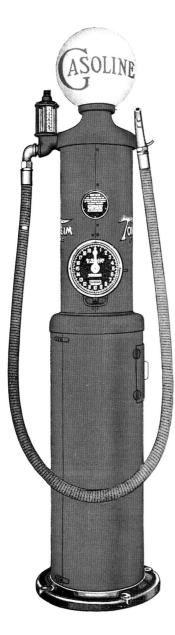

Cut 650
Manually Operated Five-Gallon Capacity Continuous Recording Pump
Equipped with Combination Hose Air Release Valve and Tele-Gauge
Speedy—Compact—Simple—Accurate—Symmetrical

Compact and symmetrical in design, this new Tokheim Five-Gallon Capacity Pump effectively fulfills every requirement for the speedy, accurate dispensing of gasoline either at the Curb or in Filling Stations.

The operation of Cut 650 requires no back-cranking, simply a continuous forward motion of the crank, which reverses the plunger at any point desired and returns it to the bottom of the stroke at a greatly increased speed. Selective quantity stops are provided for one, two, three, four and five gallons. Combination hose air release valve and tele-gauge visibly indicates whether or not the pump is in prime and insures a smooth, rapid flow of gasoline to the fuel tank of the car. The continuous recording meter—to 1,000,000 gallons and repeating—enables an accurate check to be kept on all sales. Two large continuous recording dials—located on opposite sides of the pump—afford double protection to both the customer and operator. A positive bell ringing attachment audibly indicates the delivery of each completed gallon.

This pump is approved by the Underwriters' Laboratories, Inc., and bears their label.

Tokheim Oil Tank and Pump Company
FORT WAYNE, INDIANA, U. S. A.
Offices in Principal Cities

Third Ed.   2M—1-29.

Bennett 373-B With Clock Face

By the late '20s, electric meter pumps replaced the visible units at many gasoline stations. Aptly dubbed "clock-face" dispensers, these dial units were first developed by L.O. and N.A. Carlson of Erie Meter Systems and replaced the fragile glass tank of the visible register pump for gasoline measurement. Whether flowing at fifteen gallons per minute or just one drop at a time, the new pumps boasted increased accuracy. Advanced units such as the Bennett 373-B were simpler to operate and safer than the hand-operated visible pumps. Unfortunately, these attractive "timepieces" were eventually replaced by even more practical calculator dispensers. *Courtesy Bennett Pump Company*

Cut 650 Gasoline Pumps

The Cut 650 was 1927's answer to the gasoline pump. A manually operated unit, it pumped gasoline with the continuous forward movement of a single hand crank. On each side of its symmetrical body, two large recording dials provided the means for customer and station operator to see how much gasoline was pumped, with a side-mounted "tele-gauge" provided for visual inspection of gasoline and prime condition. A long flexible filler hose, still lacking any sort of nozzle valve, provided the conduit for easy tank filling. As each gallon was cranked and delivered, an internal bell-ringing attachment provided the auditory signal. Tokheim supplied generic, round "Gasoline" globes to their 650 customers, and finished the standard model in a bright red enamel. *Courtesy Tokheim Corporation*

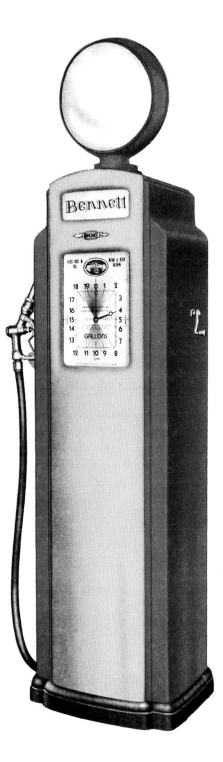

their mechanical computers radically transformed the entire pump industry. Eventually, competing pump manufacturers were forced to license the patented technology for their own pumps. Existing units were rendered obsolete—overnight.

Now, instead of reading a dial indicator for the total gallons and consulting a corresponding price chart, the operator simply glanced at the calculated price. For the first time in the history of the American service

Six Assorted Gasoline Pumps

For the last fifty years, the gasoline dispenser has been largely ignored. When Model Ts rattled up and down Main Street, visible register pump units with glass crucibles and ornate metalwork captured the public's imagination. With the introduction of graceful gas pumps, the practice of filling the family car with fuel attained a marked measure of romance and new level of style. At the Don Garlits Museum of Drag Racing in Ocala, Florida, a number of these eye-catching pumps are currently on display. Gasoline pumps, identified from left to right: Fry Ten-Gallon Model 117 visible register (circa 1916–1923) with Mobilgas Special globe, Tokheim calculator pump (circa 1950s) with Blue Sunoco Capcolite globe, Erie clock face pump with Kendall one-piece globe, Gilbarco Calco-Meter Model 906-16G with Shell one-piece cast globe, National Model A-38 (circa 1945) with Dino Capcolite globe, Fry Ten-Gallon Model 117 visible register with Shell one-piece cast globe. *Marty Lineen, Jr. © 1993, Courtesy Don Garlits Museum*

BuyFromaFry
There's One Close By!

Gasoline sellers know the famous Fry Visible Pump develops confidence and attracts business because of its dependability.

That's the reason thousands of new Frys go into use every month.

You will find it both a pleasure and a satisfaction to buy your gasoline from a service station equipped with the Fry Visible Pump.

The men in charge are dependable—so is their equipment.

Buy from a Fry—Millions do!

Guarantee Liquid Measure Co.
Rochester, Pennsylvania

PHILIP GIES PUMP COMPANY, Limited
Canadian Manufacturer and Distributor
KITCHENER, ONTARIO

Always Accurate Fry Visible

With visible register pumps such as the Fry Model 117, gasoline was pumped from an underground tank by hand lever to fill a clear glass crucible. The round glass that gave the pumping device its name was securely mounted high atop a cylindrical support base made of heavy cast iron. Alongside the cylinder wall, graduated markers descending in numerical order from top to bottom gave indication of total volume. These gallon markers read out, or "registered" the amount of gasoline pumped from the ground and stored in the glass receptacle before sale. Unfortunately, the visible-register pumps were vulnerable to cheating, since markers could easily be misaligned. The contents of the crucible often expanded when the sun heated the glass, too—causing fuel to push through an overflow valve and back into the underground tank. During the summer, purchases had to be planned for the evening or other cool periods of the day in order to obtain the most gasoline for one's money.

station, the station attendant could confidently inquire: "Shall I fill 'er-up?"

As the silhouette of the American city changed, so did the appearance of the fuel dispenser. Pumps soon mirrored architectural forms in miniature, including the key structural components indicative of modern skyscrapers.

By the close of the thirties, the characteristics of streamlining began to soften the angularity of the fuel dispenser. Industrial designers influenced by the tapered bodies of aircraft integrated the look into new products. From cars to vacuums, contoured cowling soon enveloped the mechanism of almost every machine.

Finally, gasoline pumps portrayed the illusion of speed and efficiency. They were well on their way to the future–the digital brain and remote control just around the bend.

Bennett Red 646B Pump With Spinner
The smoothing characteristics of Streamlining began to hone away the sharp edges of the American gas pump by 1939 as many industrial designers were influenced by the parabolic tails and contoured bodies of aircraft. As the hard lines of the setback idiom began to soften, a more purified style of machine aesthetic was coming into vogue. Manufacturers redesigned everything from implements to appliances, improving functionality while incorporating modern styling. Electric refrigerators became aerodynamic, vacuum cleaners more swift, and gas pumps streamlined. Contoured cowlings covering mechanical components, transforming the fuel dispenser into a minimalist box—one that conveyed the static illusion of efficiency and speed to the passing motorist.
Courtesy Bennett Pump Company

THE *Bennett* 646 B

Chapter 4

GLOBES

The practice of mounting spherical shaped billboards on top of gas pumps began shortly after the first practical fuel dispensers were perfected. Pump manufacturers inaugurated the tradition by crowning some of their early blind units with attention-getting balls.

Wayne initially proffered a simple one-piece globe in 1912 to accompany their Cut 276 gasoline pump. Crafted from molded milk-glass, its primary function was to provide a distinctly decorative look. Perched high atop a tapered post, it lent an aura of respectability to what otherwise would have been a rather unattractive machine.

At that time, the majority of representations made by these unpretentious orbs were accomplished with simple generalities. "Filtered Gasolene" became the standard inscription—first painted, then etched into heavy globe glass. Other pump makers packaged similar globes with their new fuel dispensers, constraining the details of product dispensed within the boundaries of these universal descriptions.

While the horseless carriage was still a relatively new phenomenon, employing a generic designation to market motor fuel was still an acceptable practice. When an empty gasoline tank stranded the trailblaz-

Road Runner Racer
During the 1930s, a small independent Tulsa refiner began marketing gasoline under the Road Runner brand name. On glass globes produced for Dancinger between the 1930s and '40s, the large, elongated bird is displayed in rich detail—from its oversized bill to its long graduated tail. Suspended in mid-run, the reticent roadrunner aptly conveys the idea of swiftness. Four distinct gas pump globes were manufactured during this era, including Road Runner Regular, Road Runner Anti-Knock, Road Runner 400, and Road Runner Racer. The first three designs featured a detailed black and white roadrunner across the center of the globe face. The Road Runner Racer version displays the energetic bird on the lower portion of the globe. (Road Runner, 13.5in glass, repro inserts, plastic repro body).
Red Horse Museum Collection

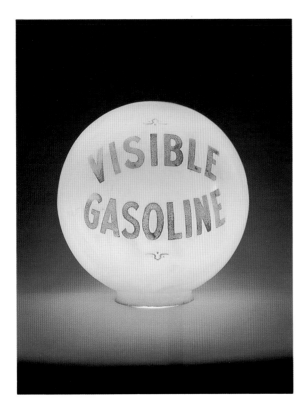

Visible Gasoline Ball
In the early 1900s, generic globes were often included by the pump manufacturer with each new unit. While unforeseen at the time, these unsophisticated glass balls became the forerunners of a massive marketing strategy poised for exploitation. Eager to gain brand recognition curbside, newly emerging oil companies lost little time in borrowing this innovation to advertise at the pumps. Soon, appealing logos and lettering were etched into rounded glass and painted with vibrant colors. Now, instead of just "Gasolene, Ethyl, or Visible Gasoline," pumps proudly proclaimed the oil company brand from atop its pinnacle. By the late '20s, a silk-screening process was used to dye the details, followed by a firing method capable of producing a baked-on finish with hues resistant to fading and the elements. Around this time, globe manufacturers refined their processes and soon raised-letter globes (cast from a mold) were available. Molded in heavy glass, these globes soon became a popular medium for displaying brands. Standard, Shell, and White Eagle were quick to see the marketing advantage of this new design and seized the opportunity—creating three-dimensional advertising for their pumps. (Generic etched glass, probable manufacturer Gilbert and Barker, circa 1912). *Red Horse Museum Collection*

ing motorist along the skirt of the roadway, obtaining combustible fluid was all that mattered–regardless of who drilled, refined, and distributed it.

As the unprecedented proliferation of the motorcar boosted the demand for fuel, the gasoline industry maneuvered into the realm of big business. To secure their share of the lucrative market, competing refiners decided to make their distillations unique. Both major and minor oil concerns soon introduced customized globes depicting individual brands of gasoline.

With the inception of colorful graphics, stylized typography, and corporate insignias, once unbranded "gasoline" transcended from a generic commodity into a highly personalized liquid. Now readily associated with the visual symbols of purity, speed, superiority, and power–it quickly assumed a myriad of new identities within the competitive realm of the roadside.

The White Eagle division of Socony-Vacuum Oil capitalized on patriotic connections deeply rooted in national pride. By using a noble bird of prey for their fuel pump globe, they instantly conjured up feelings of patriotism and strength. At gasoline stations throughout Kansas and the Midwest, proud white birds kept a watchful eye

White Eagle Globe Blunt Nosed

The symbol of the white eagle—poised in noble assertion, and chosen for its representation as an oil company name, was first produced as a gas pump globe in 1924. This one-piece Eagle cast globe captured the vision of the stately raptor while providing the Kansas refiner with a powerful symbol, easily recognizable. The commanding atmosphere attained by a group of slender pumps topped with white eagles created a robust image for the White Eagle Oil and Refining Company—a look that set the company apart from its competitors. Regarded by many as the perfect corporate symbol, the majestic eagle received several embellishments between 1924 and 1932, producing four distinct globes: the blunt-nose, the slit-throat, and two versions of the pointed-nose. Despite their subtle differences, all contributed to the effect of stately dignity at company stations throughout the Midwest. White Eagle globes are largely distinguished by the variations in bill formation and feather details. With sparse body detail, the "blunt-nose" features a rounded bill, while the "pointed-nose" versions exhibit sharply curved bills. Feathers on the molded body are far more intricate than those on the blunt nose. A later model produced in 1932 boasts remarkable body detail, setting it apart from its other pointed-nose counterparts. In regards to body and style, the slit throat could be the twin of the blunt-nose, except for the casting line around the throat. (White Eagle Oil and Refining Company, cast one-piece glass, circa 1924–1932). *White Eagle Antique Mall Collection*

on the business of refueling.

Standard Oil of Indiana introduced three-dimensional versions of a majestic crown for their pumps. When seen from the roadway by motorists, these imperial markers transmitted positive messages of aristocracy and opulence. At twenty cents a gallon, customers pumping Stanolind's IsoVis gas knew they were getting a quality fuel!

Kanotex Bondified

Inspired by the "Sunflower State" nickname, Kanotex employed the seed-rich flower of Kansas on its globes long before it was adopted as part of the Kansas state flag in 1927. Originally Superior Refining, the Midwest oil enterprise trademarked its Kanotex name in 1909. A few years later, it began availing itself of one-piece etched globes to promote product. Although a few variations developed, these early globes featured a white star placed in front of a yellow sunflower, with oversized Kanotex "O." During the '30s, the company began using globes manufactured by the Gill Glass Company of Pennsylvania. Consisting of a hollow glass body with base, the Gill featured a narrow metal band on each side used to attach glass ad panels. These inserts were secured within the metal bands with the aid of an adjustable screw. Broken panels could now be easily replaced, enabling stations to maintain their globes without the added expense of total replacement. To further enhance the beauty of their globes, Gill later added a rippled texture to the glass body. Combined with baked-on paint inside, the Gill ripple globe gave off a most pleasing glow when internally illuminated. (Total Petroleum, Kanotex, Gill/rippled glass, circa 1930–1952). *Red Horse Museum Collection*

Unfortunately, the once ubiquitous gasoline pump globe has virtually disappeared from the American scene. Modern dispenser designs have rendered pump-top advertisements obsolete and impractical. On those rare pumps that have survived the change, the specter of vandalism and theft precludes any thought of their use.

All across the endless backroads of America—along small-town main streets, little known country roads, and two-lane highways—the friendly gasoline pump globes that once glowed brightly have dimmed. The tireless beacons consigned the duty of guiding motorists to safe harbor and favorite gasoline brands ... are just a memory.

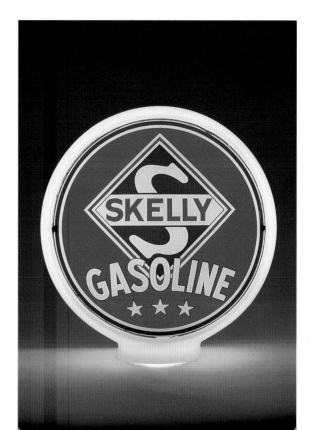

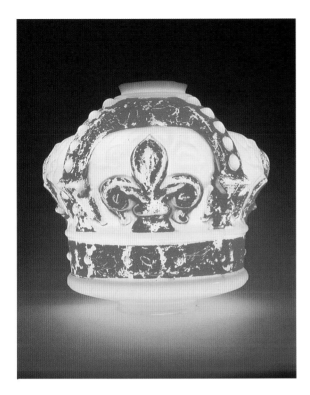

Red Crown Chimney Cap

The practical refinement of the working light bulb was fraught with pitfalls. First, there was the problem of the fragile filament. Even after an osmium version was introduced in 1902, there was a problem with longevity (they burned out after fourty hours). As a result, early electric lamps were not very reliable until after the tungsten filament was introduced in 1906. However, the bulb still became extremely hot and had a penchant to explode when overheated. To accommodate these early difficulties, globe companies manufactured a one-piece glass globe that featured a 4in opening at its top. The collar of this hole was fitted with a small metal cap, acting as both vent and removable lid. Now, built-up heat could escape easily—while protecting the bulb from the rain. As lamps continued their all-too-rapid burn out, blackened bulbs could be easily replaced by station operators—without having to remove the entire globe from the pump. During the '20s, improvements in filament coils and the use of inert gases finally created longer lasting and safer bulbs. As a result, the chimney cap globe became obsolete. (Standard Oil Company of Indiana, Red Crown, used as light/dealer promotional piece, circa 1950s). *Red Horse Museum Collection*

Opposite page, bottom
Skelly and Stars

In 1919, William Skelly pooled his vast oil holdings and founded his own personal petroleum company—promptly naming the enterprise after himself. Perceiving a climate favorable to opportunity and growth, the flamboyant Oklahoma oil man eagerly purchased numerous service stations throughout the mid-continent states. If his gamble paid off, the financial rewards would be enormous. Unfortunately, Skelly's financial demise came swiftly on the heels of the great depression. Deeply in debt, he had no choice but to relinquish control of his brainchild to Standard Oil of New Jersey. At this point, Standard found itself in control of two separate oil entities, Skelly and Tidewater. To maintain its interests and to avoid a complete merger, it formed the Mission Corporation to oversee the pair. When the powerful J. Paul Getty later gained control of Tidewater, he received both oil concerns in the deal and by the 1960s, both companies officially merged with Getty. However, Skelly still held tenaciously onto its identity, stalling complete changeover to the Getty name until well into 1983. By this time, Texaco stepped in and purchased Getty—halting the process completely. Ironically, Skelly succumbed to rebranding in 1985—under the name of yet another owner: Texaco. So it goes in the soap opera of American Gas! (Skelly Oil Company, Skelly Gasoline, 13.5in glass, circa 1950–1956). *Red Horse Museum Collection*

Phillips 66 Shield

When Adolph Spittler accidentally discovered casein plastics in 1897, the world was changed forever. Manufacturers, no longer limited to metal and glass, could now have durability, flexibility, and moldability— all in one product! Because this new plastic material could be dyed to any color during the manufacturing process, objects impervious to peeling or flaking could be readily created. As advancements were made, high heat and impact resistant acrylics, cellulose acetates, and polystyrenes went into full production by the 1930s—as did the globe manufacturers. In the forefront was the Cincinnati Advertising Products Company, of Cincinnati, Ohio. To hold glass inserts, their new plastic bodies came equipped with one screw topside and two near the base. Dubbed the "Capco," these lightweight globes were patented around 1932 and became exceedingly popular due to their durability. As the use of plastics flourished during the '50s, several manufacturers began creating unusually shaped three-piece globes. The Phillips 66 shield lent itself perfectly to this three-dimensional concept, resulting in the manufacture of two distinct models: Phillips 66 and the Phillips 66 Flite Fuel. (Phillips Petroleum Company, Phillips 66, all plastic shield, circa 1953–1959).*Dalton Patterson Collection*

Mobil Red Pump With Globe

In order to portray a more uniform brand name throughout its affiliate outlets, Socony and Vacuum (which merged in 1931) were determined to combine the Socony shield and Flying Red Horse with Vacuum's familiar "Mobilgas" brand. This conversion took many forms and was not accomplished completely until after WW II. The Magnolia and White Eagle divisions were among the first to adopt the new Mobilgas name, while others preferred to combine the Mobilgas brand designation with their own product names. As a result, globes depicting various brand names and logos— shown in concert with the Mobilgas name— proliferated. Since numerous manufacturers were involved with their design, a wide range of letter colors and type styles were seen at Socony-Vacuum affiliates, once they converted to Mobilgas. Interestingly enough, it was time for yet another rebranding in 1962 when the Mobilgas trademark was phased out.

The singular word "Mobil" replaced the old trademark, calling for replacement of gasoline pump globes one more time. Augusta, Kansas's Billie Butler has amassed quite an impressive collection of Socony collectibles. Her entire backyard is filled with Flying Red Horse signs and other Mobil memorabilia. A bright red restored Tokheim featuring a Mobilgas globe is one of her favorite pieces, occupying a position of prominence only a few feet from the edge of her backyard patio. While other neighbors play badminton and push lawnmowers through ankle high grass, Butler just sits back—takes a sip of iced tea, and admires all the colorful mementos she has acquired throughout the years. Not to be left out, husband Bob is a fan of the Flying Red Steed, too. He worked at the now defunct Mobil refinery for years and has acquired his own affection for anything and everything involved with the history of the company. *Billie Butler Collection*

Chapter 5

CONTAINERS

When Colonel Drake first punched into a reservoir of Pennsylvania crude in 1859, the storage of raw oil posed a considerable dilemma. Since exploration took up considerable time and finances, transport and packaging logistics were often left for procrastination.

Luckily, the Titusville area played host to a number of breweries. Because most of them stocked an ample supply of wooden casks to store their spirits, brew masters soon found themselves inundated by frantic oil men searching for practical receptacles. With new oil reserves discovered daily, storage barrel construction soon proved more lucrative than drilling for rock oil.

While the wooden barrel provided the first link in the chain of bringing petroleum products to market, it was far from the final solution. To accommodate the filling stations that would flourish along the nation's roadways, improved packaging methods would have to be developed.

Consequently, a variety of metal can motifs soon became standard for packaging retail auto-lubricants. Many of these oil vessels offered the convenience of a built-in pouring spout, while other designs provided

Oil Can Wall Frontal View
About twenty years ago, oil cans were generally regarded as throw-away items and were usually tossed in the trash. Those that did survive the final cut either ended up on the workbench holding screws or as a handy canister to clean dirty paint-brushes. As time progressed, a few forward thinking individuals realized that many of these tin containers featured pleasing graphics and corporate designs. Ever so slowly, a few eccentrics saved all the cans they could get their hands on and were soon scouring garbage dumps and other locations for new ones. As they worked on their new "hobby" in secret, the interest in nostalgia and filling stations increased. Suddenly, collecting oil cans was no longer a fringe activity! By the end of the eighties, desirability grew as values increased. For anyone interested in American road culture, the collecting of oil containers became serious business.
Red Horse Museum Collection

Mobiloil "A" Bottle Rack and Ford
When this 1937 Ford Tank Truck was hauling gasoline regularly, oil was often sold from clear glass decanters. A colorful rack often emblazoned with the brand name usually held eight of these bottles near a spot at the service island. The ever-ready station attendant would refill the clear one-quart containers with oil, hand-pumped from a bulk lubester capable of holding large quantities. To ensure that the customer was actually getting the quality they paid for, Mobil introduced their "Filpruf" containers. Featuring a patented spout requiring the use of a special gadget to remove it, they were filled with Mobiloil "A" at the local company bulk plant and delivered to stations for sale. (Before SAE numbers were used, different grades of oil were designated by petroleum refiners with letters. Mobil's "Guide to Lubrication" was one of the publications that outlined various grades, listing a number of formulas and their compatible make of automobile).
White Eagle Antique Mall Collection

Next page
Check the Oil Service
During the fifties, attendants at Phillips Petroleum stations made the simple procedure of "checking the oil" an integral part of the motorist's drive-in refueling ritual. Unlike the early days of the "filling station" when motor coach operators were basically on their own, vehicle owners themselves were encouraged to become part of the maintenance process. Crankcase dipsticks were readily shown to post-war customers as they were encouraged to learn all they could about their vehicle's upkeep. If the motorist himself could gain the confidence to identify oil that was breaking down, he would eventually return for an oil change and possibly the company's complete "Philcheck Service." Costly repairs would be avoided, Trop-Artic oil would be sold, and plenty of good will generated.
Courtesy Corporate Archives, Phillips Petroleum Company

a shaped metal flange to guide fluid. With the exception of cans introduced by Marathon in the shape of an oil derrick, screw-cap openings were almost universally positioned near the container's edge.

Later, a bent metal strap or heavy wire was attached to the top of these hand-soldered canisters to enable easy lifting. Rectangular full or half-gallon containers could readily be carried to a waiting motorcar by most customers.

At the same time, many gas stations sold oil from sixty-gallon bulk-dispensers positioned near the pump island. Glass bottles, usually stored in an eight container rack, were filled using the unit's small hand pump. "Fill-lines" molded into the clear bottlenecks provided the station attendant visual reference for exact quart measure.

Much to the chagrin of the public, the glass decanting method possessed gross inadequacies. Prior to the motorist's arrival, bottles could easily be filled with inferior oil, then represented as premium grade to the unsuspecting customer. As was the case with the visible register gas pumps, any visual reassurance obtained by the motorist provided a false security. Actually receiving honest measure—much less quality motor oil, wasn't always reality.

The same quandary applied to tin containers: because cans did not employ any sort of sealing device to indicate their prior opening, any disreputable seller could replenish empties with inexpensive product. Short of opening the containers upon delivery to check them, no method existed to confirm that oil purchased was actually the type and grade represented by the can label.

Eventually, a wave of allegations surfaced from a number of disgruntled sources.

Yellow Eight Car Can

The one-gallon rectangular can design was one of the earliest commercial oil vessels employed to market motor oil. Usually made of solid tin hand-soldered at the seams, these early canisters were often compact works of art. Taken for granted during their heyday as merely another form of commercial packaging, these square containers were often adorned with intricate designs. Free to embellish the metallic canvas of the oil can with engaging pictures, yesterday's unknown artists have left behind a pictorial history of packaging. During the height of their development, speedy racing cars, animals, and family sedans were the most frequent motifs employed. This one-gallon Eight Motor Oil (circa 1918) was a generic can sold to dealers and single stations empty. An operator could purchase one dozen at a time, fill them with oil, and pad stamp them to signify heavy, medium, or light grade. To unify the look of related products, identical cans were available in the one-gallon size, as well as grease containers holding one, five, and twenty-five pounds. *White Eagle Antique Mall Collection*

Good Gulf Gasoline Pump Display

This Pittsburgh Gulf station relied heavily on Wayne display case pump dispensers during the year 1933. Although extremely fragile when it came to automobiles accidentally driving into them, these glass-cased units were the perfect salesman for every manner of car accessory. *Photograph provided, and reprinted with permission, by Chevron Corporation and its subsidiary, Chevron U.S.A. Inc.*

Retailers suspected of dishonesty reportedly were not selling trusted brands as advertised. Even the popular cartoon strip "Gasoline Alley" poked fun at the problem during the 1920s.

Well aware of the effect this kind of damaging press could have on business, petroleum refiners took serious notice.

Expending considerable expense and effort, they continued to develop tamperproof packaging for motor oil. By the 1930s, most serious refiners switched to oil cans sealed at the source.

Soon, cylindrical metal tumblers filled with motor oil were sold at gas stations all across America. At long last, motorists could drive in, have the oil checked ... and be certain that the lubricants poured into their crankcases were "guaranteed to be refinery sealed!"

Oilzum Man Orange Can

The Oilzum man was an engaging trademark originated by the White & Bagley Company of Worcester, Massachusetts. Oilzum motor oils and lubrication products were quite popular during the '40s, touted on canisters as "America's Finest Motor Oils." Registered in the early 1900s as a protected product symbol, the Oilzum Man was one of America's first lubrication trademarks to become legally registered. Although quite appealing, the smirking visage was predestined for extinction from the first day it appeared on an oil can. Donning the protective headgear indicative of America's early motoring aficionados, Mr. Oilzum never failed to remind motorists of those early years. As Detroit's auto manufacturers produced more advanced machines for the post-war market, the American motorist looked increasingly towards the future—embracing the heavy chrome, streamlined fins, and modernity of the designs. Trademarks that glorified an age of antiquity quickly fell out of favor—rendered commercially impotent. In the gallery of the American marketplace, familiar characters like the Oilzum "dude" faded from prominence. Postscript: Oilzum was recently bought out by the Dryden Company of Baltimore, Maryland, and the White & Bagley headquarters in Massachusetts demolished. Believe it or not, Oilzum can still be bought in plastic bottles. *Tom Allen Collection*

Bow-tie Phillips Attendant Sells Oil

Another fanciful fable that hopes to explain the origin of the Phillips trademark is that Frank and L.E. Phillips, prior to founding the company, had only sixty-six dollars left when they struck their first successful well. Because of the timing, they decided that if they ever got to the point where they marketed gasoline it would be called "Phillips 66." This sounds believable, since the Phillips brothers were stretching their finances to the limit with their first oil explorations. After all, a fair number of dry holes were drilled by the pair prior to their first real gusher. But, whether or not they had a total of sixty-six dollars left between them when the well named Anna Anderson spouted black gold high into the Oklahoma night on September 6, 1905, cannot be confirmed by Phillips, or any other reliable historian. (Circa 1972). *Courtesy Corporate Archives, Phillips Petroleum Company*

NOW AT YOUR GULF DEALER'S _THE FINEST GULFPRIDE EVER!

The new Gulfpride keeps your engine **running better** { Gulf scientists have found new ways to cut down oxidation, carbon, varnish, and to prevent foaming. } Gulfpride is the **only** motor oil that's Alchlor-processed { This is an extra refining step. It makes Gulfpride extra pure, extra free from sludge formation. } Get the **new** Gulfpride, the world's finest motor oil!

Gulfpride Motor Oil and Station

As increased competition and a depressed economy altered the carefree climate of gas and oil marketing during the early thirties (by 1933 there were over 170,000 gasoline stations doing business in the United States), automotive lubrication services and simple mechanical repairs were looked at from a fresh perspective. Soon, "lubritoriums" were built to satisfy the demand, with many existing stations adding on hydraulic lifts or grease pits. Eventually, Gulf Oil erected magnificent Streamline Moderne structures to market their "Gulflex" lubrication services, accessories, and exterior washing-all under one roof. The undignified filling station was growing up; the complete service station design becoming its welcome replacement. Refiners were proud of their new image and weren't afraid to show it—naming improved products such as motor oil accordingly. *Photograph provided, and reprinted with permission, by Chevron Corporation and its subsidiary, Chevron U.S.A. Inc.*

Marvel Mystery Oil

The Emerol Manufacturing Company of New York captured all of the ambiance of early "snake oil" salesmen with their unique oil can packaging. For the layman, assimilating many of the fantastic claims imprinted on the can had to be done with a grain of salt (maybe even a few dozen grains). Small pyramids, cryptic slogans, and a rather intriguing circular logo all lent an aura of the unknown to this unusual contender in the arena of multi-purpose lubricants. Supposedly, no one could really account for why this lubricant was "Slicker" than others (a secret additive?) and what unique process the company employed to manufacture it. Decades before the days of synthetic oil additives and other slippery chemicals were created in a laboratory test tube, this "mysterious" substance aided tremendously in Marvel's appeal. Yet even more amazing: Marvelous Mystery Oil is still sold in auto supply stores to this day! A willful survivor from the mid-teens, it's still packaged with the same eye-catching graphics and imagery as used on the earlier containers. *White Eagle Antique Mall Collection*

White Eagle Montage

In the year 1931, a basic grease job cost only fifty cents at a Standard Oil service station. If gear lubricant was needed in the transmission or differential, it cost fifteen cents per pound. When the warmer months of the year came around, both the transmission and differential would be drained of the 90 weight gear lube and replaced by 140 weight. For the station dealers it was a profitable ritual. Like the typical oil change, the profit margins were high. At the White Eagle Antique Mall in Augusta, Kansas, owner Bob McCalla displays many typical examples of the types of containers used to store these lubricants. When the motorcar was still young, grease buckets, such as this White Eagle "Dark" Axle Grease, were a common item stocked at the filling station. *White Eagle Antique Mall Collection*

Opposite
Texaco Sky Chief Gasoline

By the 1960s, petroleum companies developed new gasolines on a continual basis, many touting secret chemical additives or revolutionary refining processes. All claimed superior performance and quality, sometimes making it difficult for the motorist unschooled in the science of chemistry to discern exactly what was flowing into their automobile's tank. Texaco introduced their Sky-Chief brand and reinforced its climate-controlled qualities with a series of prints advertising in national publications. Specially blended to deliver top performance in each of the twenty-five weather areas in the United States, this "Volatane Control" motor fuel was just the ticket " for quick starts, fast warm-ups, smooth getaways, and power-a-plenty on the highways and up the hills." *Courtesy Texaco Inc.*

PACK MORE PUNCH in your winter driving with Texaco Sky Chief. It's the only premium gasoline 100% *Climate-Controlled* in all 48 states — specially blended to deliver top performance in *your* area and in *each one* of the 25 weather areas of the U.S.A., as established by Texaco engineers. For quick starts, fast warmups, smooth getaways, power a-plenty on the highways and up the hills — it's the gasoline *for those who want the best!* So fill 'er up with Sky Chief at your Texaco Dealer, *the best friend your car has ever had!*

THE TEXAS COMPANY
TEXACO DEALERS in all 48 states

Texaco Products are also distributed in Canada and Latin America
TUNE IN . . . Metropolitan Opera broadcasts every Saturday afternoon. See newspaper for time and station.

Sky Chief
GASOLINE
TEXACO
REG T.M.

Chapter 6

SIGNS

During the dawn of America's automobile age, just hanging a hand-painted shingle by the roadside proved sufficient to peddle gas. With horse and buggy outnumbering the motorcar, the oil industry didn't require showy signs. Simple descriptions satisfied vehicle owners stranded because of an empty tank.

As the demand for gas increased and brands became important, refiners followed the lead of tobacco, soft-drink, and soap powder firms. By the turn of the century, their painted metal advertising signs already adorned a range of commercial structures—from corner grocer to ice-cream parlor. In rural towns and larger cities, businesses were covered in a patchwork quilt of incongruous advertising billboards.

While a majority of these "snipe" signs were simply painted tin, the most durable were made by fusing powdered glass onto metal sheeting with a high heat process. An extremely tough, "porcelain enameled" finish resulted, virtually impervious to wear and the destructive elements of nature. Featuring portability and ease of installation—they quickly became a hardy alternative to the

You Can Save Money Sign

Saving money has always been a major attraction for the motorist in need of a full tank of gasoline. In 1947, California independent dealer George Urich dreamed up a revolutionary new station concept targeted for California where customers could pump their own gas—pocketing the savings in the process. Initially opening three of his stations in the Los Angeles area, he forever altered the nature of the gasoline station and inadvertently set into motion a gasoline marketing controversy that would rage for years. Allowing customers to drive in and dispense fuel without the services of any sort of station attendant, Urich's new "Gas-A-Terias" consisted of eighteen to twenty-one gasoline pumps set on islands lined up at right angles to the street. Cars drove up to any one of these units in two long rows to refuel. Sometimes, patrons were parked twelve or fourteen abreast during peak periods! In the best cases, as little as two and a half minutes were required to pump gas, offering motorists the ability to refuel fast and get back on their way.

Standard Oval With Red Flame

Standard's "Torch and Oval" were once familiar players in the roadside movie. From the very early days of gas marketing until well into the mid-thirties, Standard stations were identified by either a Red Crown Gasoline sign or Polarine Motor Oil placard. From the early 1920s and on, a few of the company's products and some of the print advertising displayed the circular "Standard Oil Company Service" arrangement. This registered design incorporated a white torch with flame, positioned slightly offset over the letter "E" in "service." Around 1935, a rectangular identification sign was introduced by Standard—featuring the words "Standard Service" set within a colored field, surrounded by a thick rule. The familiar torch and oval design was adopted before the winter of 1945, although its physical implementation was hindered by post-war shortages. Fortunately, the delay proved cost-saving: before new signs could be installed, the white torch was upgraded to show off a blazing red flame. By 1948, the Standard Oil torch and flame were in full use, completely replacing the colorless version on all but product cans (they were revised in 1950).

Chevrolet Phillips 66 Sign

When the Phillips Petroleum Company introduced their new "66" gasoline during the late twenties, they didn't waste any time promoting their new product. As daring skywriters blazed across the wide blue yonder spreading the tradename of the new gasoline, company vehicles aided the public's familiarization with trunk mounted highway signs. Enlarged replicas of the familiar markers posted along Route 66, these over-sized signboards featured numerals outlined with light-catching "reflector buttons" (for maximum visability). When a car following turned on its head lamps, a moving reminder of Phillips' new motor fuel blazed a trail down the highway. *Courtesy Corporate Archives, Phillips Petroleum Company*

sign-painter's repertoire of cut pine and paint.

A perfect match for the grease and grime of the gas business, filling station operators soon contracted the services of sign makers

Flying Horse Stone With Sun

Pegasus ... Mobil's dauntless mascot—everywhere he's seen he commands attention. Striking a common chord in almost every motorist, he resonates feelings from deep within the imagination. In Greek mythology, Pegasus symbolized power and righteousness. When Perseus killed Medusa, Pegasus rose from the spilled blood. Residing in the house of the gods, he was the immortal royal steed who carried thunder and lightning for Zeus, king of the gods. For Socony (Standard Oil Company of New York) and later Mobil, the winged steed became the perfect choice to represent their products. During the '30s, renowned cowboy artist Robert Elmer took the original horse depicted here (installed above the doorway, Augusta Mobil Refinery bath house building, prior to 1993 demolition) and re-stylized it into the highly recognizable logo we know today as the "Flying Red Horse." For decades, it has been a familiar brush-stroke on the roadside canvas.
White Eagle Antique Mall Collection

and installed their own placards. Circular panels brandishing trademarks, corporate mascots, and a myriad of related pictures were proudly suspended from tall, slender poles planted close to the roadbed.

Eventually, portable versions made with supports of cast-iron were positioned in the direct line-of-sight of approaching vehicles. Often emblazoned with the likeness of a Gargoyle, Lion, or other mythical creature—matching discs of considerable diameter were installed at a place of prominence near the gable of the station structure.

To strengthen brand recognition and unify overall appearance, small reproductions of

Flying Horse on Fence Going Left

Billie Butler really loves red horses. She has a small herd corralled out in her backyard and a few of them tied up in the living room. Some of them are quite large, while others are small enough to occupy a place of prominence on top of a cabinet in her dining area. Two of her special favorites stand watch twenty-four hours per day just behind the television screen in her den. One poses on the corner of her tiny office desk. To the uninitiated, it might seem as if Mrs. Butler is in violation of local zoning ordinances and livestock laws.

But that couldn't be further from the truth! Her horses never need to be watered or curried—and mucking out a stable has never been one of her chores. For her, it's all perfectly natural. After all, the horses that share her small suburban home in Augusta, Kansas, are simply a collection of signs, statues, and plaques once used as advertising for the Mobil Oil Corporation. Butler started collecting the Flying Red Horse memorabilia years ago and has grown to love the striking symbol of speed and power. "Peggy" is definitely a part of her extended family. *Billie Butler Collection*

69

Neon Pegasus

A two-sided neon Pegasus flies above Gordon W. Smith's Mobil station in Eden Prairie, Minnesota. Smith's station was recently remodeled and lost all vestiges of its old, classic look—but the owner vowed to keep the sign as a neon crown atop his station. This is one of the last original neon Flying Horses in service in the United States. Pegasus was adopted as a trademark in the United States shortly after the organization of Socony-Vacuum in 1931, although the symbol was used as long ago as 1911. *Michael Dregni*

DX Neon Sign in Crate

The Mid-Continent Petroleum Company of Tulsa, Oklahoma, introduced their super-premium Diamond D-X brand of gasoline in the early thirties. Most of the company station outlets were rebranded with the Diamond D-X trademark by 1940. Eventually, the "Diamond" nomenclature was dropped and the D-X pair ruled station signs exclusively. Neon beauties like this red diamond sign soon lit up the roadways with their wonderful glow. Unfortunately, D-X moved towards a merger with the Sunray Oil Company in the mid-fifties, beginning the eventual demise of the geometric company symbol. In the regions where Sunoco gasoline was already being sold, the D-X name was phased out. Another gasoline brand name faded into obscurity, a hapless casualty of calculated business decisions.

these signs were permanently attached to fuel dispensers and other related service station equipment. Everywhere car customers fixed their gaze, clever phrases and flashy imagery hawked refined products. In a few years, the porcelain enameled sign became as ubiquitous as the gasoline pump.

As two-lane ribbons of asphalt became the new main streets for America, the motorist's attention span dwindled. While the pace of modern life quickened, the unpretentious advertising techniques of yesteryear began to show signs of age. Porcelain enameled signs were drained of their power to attract. The lifeless, one-dimensional placard had become commonplace—and was ultimately , taken for granted.

Fortunately, a radical advancement in sign technology caught the attention of ad executives: neon. Developed in Paris by the Claude Neon factory, Los Angeles car dealer Earle Anthony installed America's first neon sign in 1923. Outlined with clear blue tubing, his orange-red Packard show-stopper had a proven ability to slow traffic.

Soon, electrified "neon" gas illuminated signs at the service station. Shell outlined their golden seashell in yellow strips of light as Phillips 66 erected a colossal assembly of red tubing near Chicago's skyline. Socony's Flying Red Horse came to life in a blaze of glory, searing across the sky and onto the facade of the gasoline station. Petroleum companies had a new ally.

Since those unsophisticated days of horse, buggy, and hand-painted board, America's refueling outposts had, indeed, come a long, long way.

Pyro Anti-Freeze Thermometer

At one dollar per gallon, Super Pyro Anti-Freeze was one of the popular coolants available during the '30s and '40s. When Studebaker, Auburn, and DeSoto were still familiar names on the street, the ability to inhibit so-called "boil-away" at normal engine heat was an important feature. Taking its name from the Greek "Pyros," meaning heat or fire, Super-Pyro was an extremely appropriate name for an engine anti-freeze solution. For years, it was advertised with porcelain enameled signs of the variety shown here, along with another version depicting an engaging little snowman as product mascot. Still, the product moniker could not endure the test of time and eventually lost its visibility in the automotive market. As the unusual mania for starting fires became more widely recognized by its name (pyromania), a seemingly perfect brand image attained unfavorable connotations ... through no fault of its own.

Bear Service Alinement

Although not directly related to the petroleum business, yellow Bear Service signs were often (and can still be) seen attached to the wall at the corner gasoline service station. As part of the friendly pack of animals watching over the motorist, the laughing bear was always a welcome sight when the family sedan's steering wheel started to vibrate. Among the pack of wild creatures chosen to represent automotive and petroleum products, the bear takes honors as being the most common. One of the most visible examples of the bear motif was employed by California Standard: Adorning signs and other forms of advertising, their "Zerolene" polar bear poised precariously on an ice floe. Gas brands also incorporated the hibernating mammal to promote sales, capturing the motorist's imagination with brand names like "Grizzly" and "Polar." During the early '20s, the Bruin Oil and Refining Company marketed products with colorful pump globes featuring "The Bear of Them All" painted on curved glass. Continuing the trend during the '30s with their "Little Bear Gasoline," the Little Bear Oil and Refining Company ensured that the bear (as a widely used petroleum product symbol) survived for yet another generation.

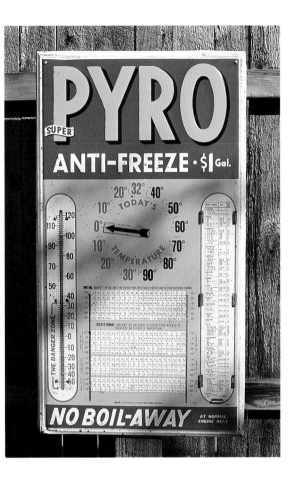

SMOKE MEANS TROUBLE!

YOU NEEDN'T tell Johnny that smoke means trouble. He knows; he's learned the hard way.

And smoke from the exhaust of your car can mean plenty of trouble, too. For smoke usually comes from excessive engine wear—wear that wastes gas and oil—wear that only costly repairs can correct.

So every time you see smoke from the exhaust of a car, let it remind you of this:

Don't wait till it's too late! Change to Insulated Havoline Motor Oil NOW—and prevent needless wear that can make your car a "smoker."

Insulated Havoline is *insulated* to stand up to high engine heats that break down ordinary oils. Free-flowing when it is cold,

Insulated Havoline prevents those dry starts which are so wearing on cylinders and pistons.

And Insulated Havoline is also distilled to remove harmful, carbon-forming impurities. Change now to Insulated Havoline. At Texaco and other good dealers everywhere.

TUNE IN FRED ALLEN—Texaco Dealers invite you to enjoy Fred Allen in the full-hour program of the TEXACO STAR THEATRE...with Kenny Baker, Al Goodman's Orchestra and a great cast. Every Wednesday Night, Columbia Network. 9:00 E.S.T., 8:00 C.S.T., 10:00 M.S.T., 9:00 P.S.T.

DISTILLED AND
INSULATED

...AGAINST HEAT ...AGAINST COLD

DON'T WAIT UNTIL IT'S TOO LATE!

Your car was never designed to "smoke." Help reduce excessive wear in *your* motor before you join America's caravan of more than 3,000,000 "smokers." Prevent smoke that results from wear by using Insulated Havoline Motor Oil.

Chapter 7

SMOKING

When automobile refueling depots were first established along the roadways of early America, an open flame was considered highly dangerous. Because gasoline was routinely spilled during the crude fillup process, fumes often posed a serious safety risk for the beginning motorist.

During the early 1900s, the routine use of above ground storage tanks only increased the hazard. Arriving automobiles often passed within a few feet of the elevated reservoirs, causing endless worry for depot operators. Any manner of spark carelessly introduced within the reach of these vapors could prove explosive—and ultimately fatal.

Later, the widespread use of curbside pumping equipment and the addition of the filling hose shifted the dangers. The ritual of refueling an automobile moved from the sparsely populated outskirts of town to the higher density of the inner city.

By then, safety levels were increased only marginally. The introduction of underground holding tanks was a welcome improvement, but technical enhancements designed to protect against the fire threat demanded refinement.

While the introduction of the visible register gasoline pump promised a new lev-

Smoke Means Trouble

At the American service station, smoke meant trouble in more ways than one! According to early Texaco ads for their distilled and insulated Havoline Oil, automobiles were never "designed to smoke." Excessive motor wear caused by inferior lubrication products was the usual culprit behind sick vehicles, easily avoided by filling the crankcase with the right kind of motor oil. Discouraging little Johnny from experimenting with tobacco products was not quite so easy—but, provided the perfect advertising association to remind the motorist of what an engine might feel like if infiltrated with too much smoke. Still, in an age when oil companies were distributing matchbooks imprinted with their own advertising, it seems curious that a magazine ad would depict fire sticks in such a negative setting. *Courtesy Texaco Inc.*

Rolex Esso Lighter

Walking Billboard, Inc. of Chicago was one of the most visible manufacturers of cigarette lighter advertising pieces. By imprinting brand names and slogans on small, personal objects, their aim was to promote the sale of goods and services in ways conventional advertising could not. While a large sign lit with bright chase lights was a highly visible way to sell, it was too large to fit inside a purse or pocket. As portable ads, quality lighters (similar to this Rolex model) fit the bill. Ever since the dissolution of the Standard Oil Trust in 1911, legal restrictions have halted any company from using the Standard name (or the Esso derivative) on a national basis. As a result, the Esso brand introduced in 1926 was used in the East, Humble in Ohio, and Enco in other regions. Unfortunately, this made it difficult for Standard to achieve name recognition nationally. During the early '70s, the decision makers at Esso decided that a name change was in order—dubbing the top-secret project Operation Nugget. To guarantee security, top level executives typed their own memos and letters. The Enco name was considered, but quickly eliminated after further study (it meant "stalled car" in Japanese). Thousands of possibilities were investigated and a computer was employed to generate a list of meaningless letter combinations. After testing some of the final names in fifty-five languages and interviewing over 7,000 customers, the new identity was finally selected. A computer creation tailor-made for worldwide use was the winner: Exxon (the double "x" occurred only in the Maltese language)! Estimated cost for the entire name change project: $100 million. *Gyvel Young-Witzel Collection*

Skelly Matches and Book

The Skelly Oil Company decided to move against the popular norm by distributing stick matches (packaged within an under scale replica of a one-quart oil container) to its gasoline customers. Unlike most ordinary paper matches, these gold-tipped beauties left a most memorable impression with the discerning gasoline customer. To this end, the bold Skelly insignia and corporate colors played a large role in their external packaging. By today's safety standards, it's hard to believe that incendiary sticks like this were ever distributed by gasoline businesses. When burned, wooden match sticks of this type have a tendency to remain hot—even moments after their flame burns out. Consider the possibilities: If carelessly tossed out of a car window within the vicinity of gas pump's vapors or flicked into a rubbish bin near the oil can rack—a smoldering match stick could easily turn a refueling stop into a disaster area. *White Eagle Antique Mall Collection*

Phillips Cigarette Lighter
As an attention-getting alternative to paper matchbooks imprinted with advertising, refiners like the Phillips Petroleum Company joined other companies by distributing fancy cigarette lighters decorated with their corporate colors and trademark. Unlike the plastic throw-away versions offered for sale at the cash registers of today's mini-markets, these distinctive flame throwers were substantial units— proudly displayed and coveted by all of the smokers lucky enough to own one. As inhabitants of today's "throw-away" society, it's sometimes hard to imagine that only a few decades ago, ordinary sundries like the fountain pen, cigarette lighter, drinking cup, soft-drink bottle, and razor were used repeatedly—until they became completely unusable and needed permanent replacement. As more and more of our natural resources become depleted, the reusable attitudes of a previous generation are being rediscovered.

el of honesty, the mechanism employed to terminate fuel flow remained impractical. The standard gas pump filler hose still did not feature any type of hand-actuated flow valve at the end. A valve mounted on the pump unit controlled fluid release.

Motorists routinely miscalculated their tank's holding capacity, often resulting in excess gasoline spillage. For those fearless enough to indulge in the habit of smoking a cigar while topping off, the end was literally close at hand.

Fortunately, petroleum refiners began regulating these unsupervised procedures. Station equipment eventually became off-limits to motorists as full-time pump attendants shouldered the responsibility for refilling gas tanks. Signs were posted near pumps to warn against smoking and customers routinely instructed to kill their engines before service. Experienced servicemen ensured that all manner of flame was extinguished and that proper safety precautions were followed. Careless customers driving in with lit cigarettes dangling from their lips were immediately warned to extinguish them.

To re-ignite their stogies, smokers often visited the local drugstore and utilized the free gas flame provided at the cigar counter. Eventually, gasoline pump operators working along Main Street took notice. Those with foresight immediately recognized a new avenue for promoting their services.

Bowing to increased pressure from the matchbook salesmen, independent stations

Standard Ashtray with Patches
For the road traveler enamored of souvenirs from a trip, the basic ashtray has always proven itself quite popular. Major and minor tourist attractions sold (and still sell) them in large quantities along virtually every roadway in the country. Of course, a few business establishments serving the motorist use them purely for the purpose they were intended: to catch ashes falling from a lit cigarette and to hold their smoldering remains. Regardless of their use, one fundamental question has been endlessly debated by travelers down through the years: if an ashtray depicting advertising (text and images) is "appropriated" from a roadside business such as a hotel, restaurant, or gas station— is it theft? Aren't these glass receptacles placed there for the sole purpose of advertising? While the answer to this weighty question may never be found, the fact remains that the ashtray is the perfect, portable memento of long-distance road excursions.
Steve Perrault Collection

soon signed orders for books printed with their name and location. Major petroleum refiners followed. Eventually company stations and local operators all over the country were freely distributing the very means to their destruction.

In what seemed like a curious marriage, the gasoline refueling station and the matchbook became partners. The most feared enemy of the gasoline proprietor was now an important part of the overall advertising scheme.

Soon advertising by way of matchbook was regarded as a viable portion of the typical station's marketing. Not only were these minuscule billboards practical, they proved an economical way to promote gas brands. A colorful advertisement provided an instant reminder of where to refuel every time the motorist went to light up a cigarette.

Opposite
Buddy, Can You Spare a Light?

Today, gasoline station advertising matchbooks exist as miniature windows into America's gas station glory days. Rife with the potent imagery of customer service, quality, unbridled speed, everlasting power, and convenience—they are clear evidence of this nation's love affair with the automobile. Despite warnings from the Surgeon General, the relationship between cigarettes, the American highway, and the gasoline service station remains as strong as it ever was. To the chagrin of the modern motorist in search of scenery, an endless procession of billboards hawk almost every brand of smoke—along virtually every mile of roadway. To augment these roadside messages, matchbooks continue to be passed out freely—the innocent themes popularized by yesteryear's gas businesses superseded by the cool attitudes of Joe Camel. Gone are the naive depictions of station attendants and carefree couples out for a Sunday drive. *Michael Witzel © 1993, Matchbooks from Steve Perrault Collection*

Shur-Stop Fire Grenades

During the 1930s, a number of American chemical manufacturers produced some extremely physical examples of commercial fire fighting equipment. Companies like the Red Comet Company, Red Ball, and the International Fire Equipment Company manufactured and marketed sealed glass "grenades," filled with crimson-colored carbon tetrachloride. Usually, six of these chemical grenades were packed within a portable case, similar to this Shur-Stop kit. When a fire broke out at the gas station, restaurant, or factory, these hand-held crucibles were thrown into the flames by the nearest bystander. When the glass broke, the carbon-tetrachloride quickly inhibited further combustion. Although quite effective in some situations, they could be totally useless against combustion already firmly established. Most of the fire grenades were of the throw type, while some featured built-in pot metal with a heat-activated spring and plunger device. Offered in a wide assortment of decorative glass and fancy holders, some were suspended from the ceiling or attached to the wall. When external heat reached a certain temperature, fluid would automatically spray onto the fire. Utilized widely at various commercial enterprises (including gasoline stations), carbon-tetrachloride grenades enjoyed a short-lived popularity before the advent of the more practical, and highly effective, dry-chemical extinguishers in use today. *Frank J. Liska Collection*

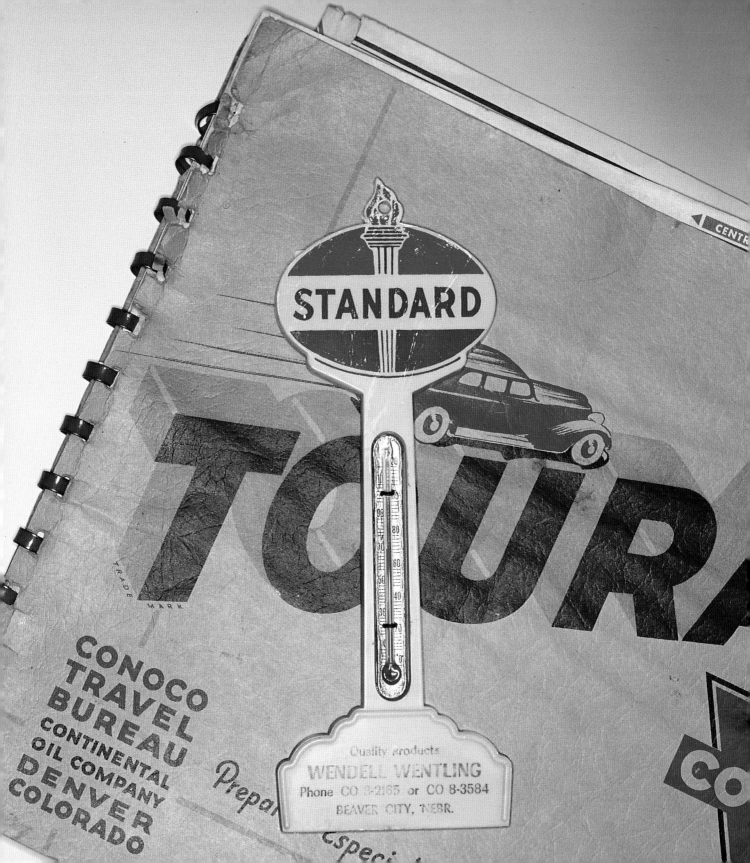

STANDARD

Quality Products
WENDELL WENTLING
Phone CO 8-2165 or CO 8-3584
BEAVER CITY, NEBR.

CONOCO
TRAVEL
BUREAU
CONTINENTAL
OIL COMPANY
DENVER
COLORADO

Chapter 8

PREMIUMS

In 1914, the mortar on Gulf's first Pennsylvania service station wasn't even dry when advertising man William Akin suggested the company mail road maps of Allegheny County to all of its registered motorists.

Ten-thousand guides were delivered without charge, resulting in a pleasant surprise for many local car owners. Since existing roadways were poorly marked and written directions cumbersome, road maps were regarded as a practical and useful gift.

Many delighted recipients responded with their cars at the pumps. Business boomed and station attendants began handing out even more road maps. Soon, guides featuring the surrounding states were printed as new customers associated generosity with the "Sign of the Orange Disk."

Other oil concerns quickly followed Gulf's lead. By the mid-twenties, virtually every major refiner offered maps–and other free goods to their customers. Products were now a major part of the promotional equation, including license plate emblems, paper radiator shields, glassware, fountain

Standard Oil Sign Thermometer
When all of the petroliana (gas and oil collectibles) currently available have been collected, what will be left for future treasure hunters? Are some of the gasoline advertising and promotional goods being distributed by today's quickie marts worth stashing away for a future collection? Will sports bottles, drink cups, and other ordinarily mundane retail items become the gas station heirlooms of tomorrow? Could a plastic Früsen Gladjen container someday be worth something? It's anyone's guess. After all, who could have predicted thirty years ago that a Standard Oil sign made into a miniature plastic thermometer would someday be worth a twenty dollar bill? No one can accurately gauge the possible worth of any object in the future, much less make a more than educated guess at what kind of item that might be. What about Batman memorabilia, pizza delivery boxes, gum wrappers, Star Wars toys, and trash can liners: tomorrow's treasures? Stick around a few more decades, only then will we know for sure!
White Eagle Antique Mall Collection

Put a Tiger in Your Tank Toy

"Put a Tiger in Your Tank" was one of the gasoline industry's most memorable slogans. For Esso (changed to Exxon in 1972), the dynamic orange feline was the perfect match for Mobil's Flying Red Horse. Like Pegasus, the black-striped mascot symbolized speed, agility, and power—a potent combination to represent gasoline and automotive products. But that's where the similarities between the Tiger and the Flying Red Horse ended: pleased with the positive effect of their down-to-earth trademark, Standard Oil of New Jersey (Esso) released a number of station premiums and promotional toys in support of the striped beast. Along with the usual key-chains and knick-knacks, a fur covered tiger with wind-up motor shuffled into the hearts and minds of young and old service station visitors. Factoid: Many of the old-time executives from the Powerine Company (bought out by Standard Oil of New Jersey) attest to the fact that their original tiger trademark inspired the entire Esso campaign. Reportedly, the advertising idea was developed in Europe first, where the feline was reworked into a cartoon format. Soon after the promotional campaign became a proven winner overseas, the concept was brought back to the states and introduced to American gasoline consumers.
White Eagle Antique Mall Collection

White Eagle
Balanced Ethyl
Gasoline
and
Keynoil
The Original
High Compression Motor Oil

**Free Air and Water, Reliable Road Information
Clean Rest Rooms—To Enjoy Your Trip**

White Eagle Balanced Gasoline and Keynoil

Previous page
White Eagle Station With Autos
During the twenties and thirties, the automobile road maps and travel guides passed out free of charge to customers were often colorful showcases for all manner of art. Scenes rife with motor vehicles, aircraft, station attendants, gasoline pumps, trademark signs, bucolic landscapes, and cars full of passengers made it onto the tri-fold covers of these handy commercial booklets. The adventurous fun and whimsy of motoring over America's roadways became their dominant theme, combined with the boundless good nature of the neighborhood service station operator and his pumping staff. While the oil company road map may have been a useful tool, it served a greater purpose: popularizing the notion of motor travel for pleasure, vacations taken by car ... and the unbridled consumption of gallons of gasoline. *White Eagle Antique Mall Collection*

Shell's Anti-Screwdriver Crusade
During the latter part of the thirties, Shell Oil Company service stations became headquarters for a nationwide Share-the-Road Crusade. According to traffic authorities, twenty-five percent of all Stop-and-Go was caused by thoughtless, selfish drivers—by "Screwdrivers." When motorists drove into the local "Show your colors" Shell station, they would receive a free booklet that illustrated these careless driving mistakes and how to improve them. In addition, a friendly service station attendant would attach a free Share-The-Road emblem to the customer's automobile license plate. Not only would the colorful insignia and colored flags inform others that you were doing your part to eliminate careless driving, it sold gasoline, too. As the booklet stated: "For the Stop-and-Go driving that can't be avoided, we recommend Super-Shell. With Super-Shell and 'Share-the-Road,' everybody saves!" *Courtesy Shell Oil Company*

pens, toys, matches, lens-tissue, fans, ink-blotters, hand-lotion, and even replica service stations.

While air for the tires and water for the radiator were recognized as helpful service station amenities, they lacked the pizzazz required to capture the imagination of the modern vehicle owner. Filling stations that distributed entertaining trinkets and automotive accessories were remembered. Gifts showered upon the wife and children commanded lasting attention–the kind that cemented true brand loyalty miles on down the highway.

Some giveaways were in exchange for repeated patronage, others simply for driving in to have the oil checked. Many premiums related directly to the gasoline or lubricant marketed, while others bore no association at all. The complimentary gift was often not as important as its intended message: This service station establishment and parent company care enough about the customer to give him more than he bargained for.

Historically, the majority of these petroleum giveaways functioned purely as vehicles for advertising. Highly visible, the phone number and address of the participating gasoline dealer almost always appeared somewhere on the gratis object. Paper-based merchandise such as hand-held fans, children's games, and small thermometers provided the perfect medium for printed promotions.

In many cases, the complimentary goods bore only the trademark of the parent company or insignia of a particular gasoline brand. Sometimes, objects themselves were modeled after a real-life piece of

WITH THIS EMBLEM—SHOW YOUR COLORS!

Join this crusade against "SCREWDRIVERS"
-help cut STOP-and-GO 25%

WE Shell dealers have started something! In addition to selling Super-Shell, the gasoline which cuts the *cost* of Stop-and-Go, we're headquarters for the nation-wide Share-the-Road crusade to cut the *amount* of Stop-and-Go!

Traffic authorities say 25% of all Stop-and-Go is caused by thoughtless, selfish driving—by "Screwdrivers."

The *Share-the-Road* Club is out to correct this condition. Public opinion can curb "Screwdrivers"—cut Stop-and-Go 25% right now!

SHOW YOUR COLORS—come in and we'll attach the Shell Share-the-Road emblem to your car FREE. We'll give you a booklet that shows the boners "Screwdrivers" pull.

For the Stop-and-Go driving that *can't* be avoided, we recommend Super-Shell. With Super-Shell and "Share the Road," *everybody* saves!

WIDE-MODEL "SCREWDRIVER"—20 miles an hour is his pace—but you need an airplane to pass him! A line of cars jams up behind, and needless Stop-and-Go results . . . Remember, your engine uses *3 times* as much gasoline in low and second gears as in high—when a "Screwdriver" forces you to shift gears, *you pay!*

"Share the Road" and SUPER-SHELL both save on STOP-and-GO

87

service station equipment. Many premiums were reproductions of corporate mascots, intended for permanent display on the family flivver.

Like the prize at the bottom of the Cracker-Jack box, the gas station premium was that little extra value we motorists looked forward to when purchasing our gasoline. Whether a coin bank fashioned in the form of a diminutive oil can or pair of petite gasoline pumps intended for salt and pepper, their prime intention was to remind us where the most generous gasoline dealer on the boulevard could be found.

A tiny uniformed Esso man or transistor radio disguised as a car battery might not have been something we really needed, but it sure was fun when it was handed to us... for free.

Pegasus License Placard Route 66

Mobil's license plate ornament embossed with the Flying Red Horse mascot is one of the genre's most graphic. A number of different versions were manufactured, including types to promote safe driving, patriotism, and even the California World's Fair. From today's perspective, these engaging placards illustrate just how radically different automotive designs were during the years when bumpers were made of metal and dashboards trimmed in wood. It used to be that the tail end of an automobile protruded far from the rear of the chassis. Trunks were often enormous affairs, usually large enough to hold the luggage for an entire family. The area for license plate mounting was an uncomplicated affair, with plenty of extra clearance available to attach any number of placards handed out by businesses. Unfortunately, new body styling and the radical redesign of bumpers caused the prominence of the license plate mounting area to wane, rendering these colorful advertising placards obsolete.

Mobilgas Salt & Pepper

During the age of limitless service station premiums, Salt & Pepper shakers were manufactured by novelty companies for the major refiners. Inexpensively molded from plastic, these branded giveaways proved a practical and economical method to increase patronage. With their compact design, they provided the retailer with a clever means by which to infiltrate the suburban home. An endless supply of these inexpensive spice dispensers were routinely distributed to regular customers—eventually finding their place on top of dinette tables. Once firmly established and accepted as another household object, the unassuming shakers would work their magic. When breakfast, lunch, or dinner called for additional flavor, the oil refiner's trademark was there—ready to serve. Later, when a dipping fuel gauge called for gas, the subconscious did the rest. Tasty memories became the gas station's asset. *Gary Rawlings Collection*

HEY, KIDS!

It's simple to own one of the keen scale model Mobilgas Tank Trucks illustrated on this card.

Because we are anxious to meet you and your folks and acquaint them with our brand of service, we are offering you a free scale model Mobilgas Tank Truck.

Just get Mom or Dad to drive into our station today and fill up with Mobilgas "R" or Mobilgas Special. Every time they purchase 5 gallons we will mark off one of the 5-gallon squares shown on purchase card in upper right-hand corner.

When all squares shown on this card have been marked off by us (representing purchase of 40 gallons) this scale model Mobilgas Tank Truck will be *yours* absolutely free.

So get started on your fleet of trucks today. Ask the folks to drive in and fill up with Mobilgas. There's no limit to the number of these trucks you can own. We have them in stock now! — See you soon!

MOBILGAS TANK TRUCK PURCHASE CARD

*DEALER

5	5	5	5	5	5	5	5

CUSTOMER'S NAME

DATE

Actual Photo of Mobilgas model Tank Truck

Mobilgas Red Oil Tanker on Wood

Mobilgas service stations rewarded loyal customers with scale replicas of company tank trucks (like this tin example) at most of their retail outlets during the forties and fifties. For the lucky baby-boomer riding shotgun, anticipating the next filling station prize was a thought eclipsed only by the images of cheeseburgers and ice cream cones. To pass the time while motoring down one of America's limitless highways—there was nothing like having a brand new service station premium to play with. "Ask the folks to drive in and fill up with Mobilgas, there's no limit to the number of these trucks you can own. We have them in stock now—see you soon!" *Billie Butler Collection*

90

Mobilgas Truck Card

When parents couldn't be convinced to visit the local service station, youngsters were often employed to coax their elders in for other purposes. Premium offers like this Mobilgas tank truck promotion were a successful way for refiners to increase patronage and ensure repeat business. Once the parent/vehicle owner pumped his or her first five gallons of gasoline, they were effectively hooked! From then on, the copilot in the back seat would take hold of the purchase card and begin to dream—bound and determined to remind the one behind the wheel where to refuel once the gas gauge dipped into the empty zone.
Red Horse Museum Collection

Plastic Shell Truck

Everyone knows that toy cars and trucks rank extremely high in the pecking order of children's favorite toys. The desire for a new model or type can be so strong for a small child that he or she would do anything to persuade his or her parents to visit the toy store or business where they might be purchased. Service stations were in tune to this fact early on and began to offer colorful tin-trucks as attractive incentive items. Some were given away with no strings attached at special grand-openings and promotions, while others required parents to fill up with a pre-determined amount of gasoline before a punch card could be redeemed for the multi-wheeled prize. Shell, Mobil, Gulf, Sinclair, and a host of other oil refiners offered a wide variety of these toy gasoline tankers. Yet, unlike some of the other features of the American gas station that have fallen by the wayside, the concept of the scaled-down gasoline tanker still lives. Texaco promotes a new model every year, much to the delight of today's generation of young truckers.
White Eagle Antique Mall Collection

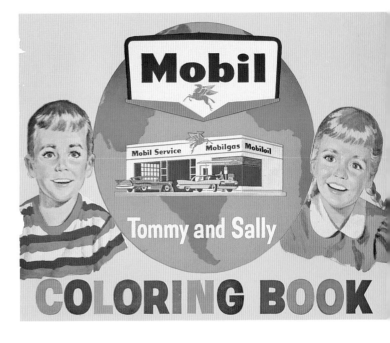

Tommy and Sally Coloring Book

To capture the attention of the automobile's youthful passengers, petroleum refining companies like Mobil Oil printed coloring books to be passed out as promotional give-aways. Inside, outlined pictures depicted the various ways company products were refined, marketed, and ultimately used. With crayons, children would fill in the colors of a service attendant's uniform, station buildings, and refining facilities—in effect, producing their own paper advertising materials. Sure to remind them of their favorite gas station once they reached driver's license age, the coloring book was a clever medium for training future generations of automobile owners where to go for service, value, and quality.

Phillips 66 Give-Away Montage

Phillips Petroleum was one of many gasoline refiners that offered premium gifts to everyday customers. When the time came to refill the gas tank, a friendly station attendant could always be counted on for another interesting trinket. Young and old alike looked forward to their next service station visit, eager to receive the goodies produced from the pockets of the pump operators. Small souvenirs such as key-chains, plastic letter openers, and ice-scrapers could be manufactured economically in large quantities—making them a perfect choice for gratis distribution. Of course, the imprinted brand name and station location played a large role in the effectiveness of these baubles. Free premium goods were (and still are) a potent form of good will advertising, free from the annoying repetitiveness of jingles and overly familiar slogans. *Red Horse Museum Collection*

RAIN GAGE

KOCHENDERFER OIL COMPANY

Phillips 66
Philheat

Cochrane, Wisconsin

2235

Texaco Fire-Chief Toy Hat

In an attempt to offset the economic effects of the "great" depression, Texaco introduced its Fire-Chief Gasoline in 1932. To inaugurate the new addition, comedian Ed Wynne (known over the airwaves as the "Perfect Fool") kicked off a full-scale comedy radio program—broadcast from coast-to-coast on the NBC network. As the first large-scale radio show to raise a glass curtain between the audience and performers (and broadcast live), the Texaco Fire-Chief show proved to be an effective promotional vehicle for the company's new automotive gasoline. To heighten the public's awareness of the new motor fuel and to further exploit the "fire" theme, Texaco later offered plastic firefighter hats at dealer outlets. Boxed with the familiar "You can trust your car to the man who wears the star" slogan emblazoned on cardboard, they quickly became the ultimate delight for many youngsters. With a battery powered microphone and small loudspeaker embedded into the helmet front, they provided the imaginative firefighter-to-be hours of fun. *White Eagle Antique Mall Collection*

Phillips 66 Banks and Rain Gauge

Along with rain gauges and other sundry gadgets, personal coin banks became a popular give-away item for petroleum refiners. Most notably, the so-called "fatman" coin bank (made of plastic) became a favorite among gasoline marketers, many utilizing the rotund example shown in this lineup as a station premium. Complete with molded attendant's hat, standard uniform, black bow-tie, shined shoes, and beaming grin—these diminutive money receptacles consolidated all of the features of the station pump jockey into one portable package. Along with the circular style banks made in the miniaturized shape of a one-quart oil container, they became effective advertisements for all manner of product and services. Holding the customer's loose change constituted only a small part of their important job. *Red Horse Museum Collection*

S&N
GREEN STAMPS

America's Most Valuable Stamps

THE SPERRY AND HUTCHINSON COMPANY
ESTABLISHED 1896

S&H Green Stamp Booklet

Anyone who has ever eaten at a roadside hamburger stand with carhop service or chomped on popcorn at a drive-in movie theater knows what S&H Greenstamps are. At businesses all across America, proprietors once passed out these small green booklets to customers. Whenever a retail purchase was made at participating establishments, ribbons of perforated stamps were distributed—in direct proportion to the total cash amount of the customer's purchase. As stamps were accumulated, they were licked and pasted inside booklets, until all of the pages were filled. Completed booklets were traded for merchandise (toasters, lawn furniture, bicycles) at redemption centers located in various regions of the country. American consumers quickly took to this added incentive program and service stations eagerly embraced the clever rebate system. Established in 1896 by the Sperry and Hutchinson Company, Green Cooperative Cash Discount Stamps were once a familiar part of buying gasoline.

Flying Horse Key-Chain

A large majority of petroleum concerns passed out free key-chains as station premiums. Among the roster of products available, these diminutive freebies often provided the most cost-effective solution in the arena of complimentary incentive gifts. The key-chain was a perfect choice for promotion, too. It was easily carried, highly useful, and performed a very important task: keeping car keys organized and in one place. Some of the more useful versions incorporated plastic coin holders, nail clippers, and even pen-knives. One unusual model distributed by Socony and others featured a small tube with enough space inside to store a rolled-up driver's license or emergency cash! Not surprisingly, a few oil refiners went one step further than the basic key-chain by offering actual key blanks featuring their company logo. The automobile ignition key could now feature the owner's favorite brand! *Red Horse Museum Collection*

Index